THE

POWER

WITHIN

*A complete habit formation guide for
the busy minds in a frantic world.*

A 21 DAY MEDITATION
CHALLENGE

ANURAG RAI

Founder of Superhuman In You

www.superhumaninyou.com

The Power Within

SUPERHUMAN IN YOU
www.superhumaninyou.com

I like to dedicate this book to you, the reader. Most of you may not have heard of me before. Yet if you are reading this page, it shows your commitment to grow, your desire to learn, and your curiosity to discover your unlimited potential. You are a seeker, and that is what inspires me to share any little wisdom I have.

"Everything in our world is made up of energy. Practicing meditation increases our awareness of energy within and around us so that we can deal with all challenges in life at the energy level."

– Anurag Rai
(Founder - Superhuman in You)

Contents

A Personal Note from the Author

Hello, and Welcome. My name is Anurag. I have been practicing meditation for over ten years; still, you may find that I am not your traditional meditation teacher, and this book is not your classic meditation book. The world around us has changed, and going away from the material world and meditating on a mountain is simply not viable for most of us. Hence, we need a practice that is for our age and still brings the same benefits. Now you may ask why bother to meditate? And what's all this buzz about?

Over the last few decades, our technology has grown way faster than our consciousness. We live in a world that is connected yet so disconnected. We experience continuous stress on our bodies and mind in our advanced society. Why? Simply because our bodies and brains are not designed to live in high-rise buildings, eat food from microwaves, travel on airplanes, stare at screens all day, and other million things we do in the modern world. However, these things have become essentials of our life, and it's impossible to take them out of our lives. It is, therefore, vital in today's world that we use a practice such as meditation to take a break and recharge.

Most of us are either working on improving our physical fitness or at least have intentions of doing so. Yet not many of us have ever given a thought about our mental fitness. We all want a chiseled figure, six-pack abs, and strong arms. But what about having a strong mind, without which everything else will become useless. There is only so much one can build with strong arms, but there is no limit to what you can build with a strong mind.

Research shows that regular meditation can not only heal your mind but also make it happier, healthier, and stronger. Meditation is the fastest and the only way to upgrade your state of consciousness. If you are not meditating, you are not using your full potentials. I urge you not necessarily for me but for you to listen to your inner voice and turn off your skepticism. I do not want any fear or doubt to stop you from living this amazing journey. The book you are holding was written in a year but was created in a decade. Use this book as a guide for the next 21 days, and I promise you that these 21 days will bring a permanent shift in the way you think and live.

I invite you to discover a life of freedom, a life of joy, and a life of unlimited possibilities.

Anurag

Introduction

I am thrilled that you have chosen to buy this book and guarantee you that your life will never be the same again if you practice the techniques described in this book with full dedication. Meditation is just like any other skill you may have developed, the more you practice, the better you get at it. I want to make this clear that there is no such thing as a good or bad meditation. It is about experiencing the journey, and there is no destination. As you continue your practice, you will experience beautiful states of the mind. It is, however, essential to do it consistently as a daily ritual.

You will notice that some chapters may not be directly related to meditation as most of us perceive it (sitting on a mat with your eyes closed). This is because I want to introduce you to some other models/concepts which have helped me face everyday life challenges and remain positive. These concepts and practices will also help accelerate the benefits of your meditation practice.

So, let's start this journey by making promises to each other. My promise to you is that if you are not happy with this book, you can get a full refund of the money you paid. No matter where you got this book from, just email me directly at *anurag.rai@superhumaninyou.com*. In return, I want you to promise to yourself that you will give all you got to follow the steps in this book with full honesty and without any procrastination for the next 21 days. You may be thinking, why 21 days? According to research, it is found that it takes 21 days to form any new habit. Therefore, the idea is that if you followed this program with full dedication for the next 21 days, you would create one of the most rewarding habits of your life.

The structure of each one of the 21 chapters in this book will be similar. Every session will have 10 -15 minutes of me explaining to you a new concept for that day, followed by 10 minutes of guided or silent meditation. You can download the mp3 version of guided meditations from www.superhumaninyou.com. Follow the steps below to access your Book Bonuses.

1. Go to the website link above. And click on the account icon in the top right corner of the web page. See below.

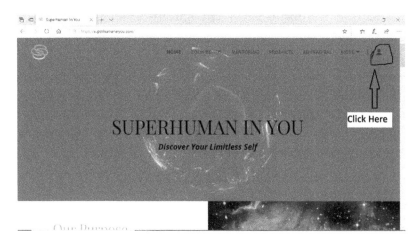

2. Select the option - 'Create Account' from the drop-down list. Enter your details and click submit.
3. You will receive an email within minutes to activate your account. If it's not in your inbox, check your junk mail.
4. Click on the link in the email to activate your account. If you have received the email in your junk folder, you

may need to move it to your inbox before you can click the link.

5. Once you click the link, you will be asked to set up a password.
6. Once you set your password, you are ready to go. You can access all your bonus content by navigating to the Book bonus tab on the website or by visiting this link www.superhumaninyou.com/book-bonus

Please join the Private Facebook group exclusive for the readers of this book, at www.facebook.com/groups/21daysmeditationchallenge. You can ask questions and support each other here.

At the end of each chapter, you will find a small action step to take for the day. I would recommend that you read all chapters in the sequence. We all are different and have different belief systems, but to take full advantage of this book, I urge you to approach each concept with an open mind. Try everything, and once you finish the book, you can pick and choose the practices that benefitted you the most.

I hope you are as excited as me. Let's begin.

Day 1
A Brief History of Meditation

"When there is harmony between the mind, heart, and resolution, then nothing is impossible."

- Rig Veda

Meditation has only become popular in the last century, although the practice itself is older than 4000 years. The Earliest written records of meditation (Dhyana) are found in Vedas from India. Ancient philosophy suggests that the purpose of human life is self-realization, and meditation is the only path that leads to this goal. Bhagavad Gita, a scripture from prehistoric India, recommends meditation as the most effective tool for controlling the human mind. Different practices of meditation were developed in Taoist China and

Buddhist India around 6th century B.C. Chakra and Mantra meditations originate from Vedas and Mindfulness meditation techniques come from Buddhist philosophy.

Meditation was mainly considered a religious or spiritual practice by most people until the early years of the 20th century. However, the last few decades have seen an increase in the experiments performed by neuroscientists, and we now have strong scientific evidence to prove the various physical and psychological benefits of practicing meditation. I will discuss these in the next chapter. For now, let's explore what meditation is?

What is Meditation?

There are different ways of explaining what meditation is. The world around us has too much unnecessary noise. I like to define meditation as a super-practice to cancel this noise, so you can use all your energy and be more healthy, productive, and aware. Think about it as if our mind is a computer, whenever we have a new thought or event, we open a new window. Now throughout our life, we keep on opening new windows. Have you ever noticed that when you have too many windows opened, your computer slows down? This is exactly what's happening with our brain. By making meditation as a part of our daily ritual, we can close any unnecessary windows, hence freeing up the energy to use for essential activities. I will talk more about the different kinds of meditation practices on Day 9. Thank you for showing up today, and let's do our today's meditation.

Meditation Day 1
Breathing Meditation (Anulom Vilom)

This technique of meditation is beneficial to balance your nervous system and release any stress from the body. There are several ways you can do this technique. A variation of this technique is also referred to as Box Breathing.

Left to left nostril is breathing technique where we breathe in from our left nostrils and then breathe out from the left again while closing the right nostril with our fingers. In Patanjali yoga sutras, this technique has been referred to as Chandrabhedi Pranayama and is considered as a water dominated *asana,* which has a cooling effect on the body. It activates the right side of the brain and is excellent in relieving hypertension, excessive heat, and relaxing the nervous system. The opposite is **right-to-right** nostril breathing known as Suryabhedi Pranayama. As the name suggests, this technique is fire dominated and heats the system. **Anulom Vilom** combines the benefits of these two asanas and is very useful in bringing the body at balance.

To perform Anulom Vilom, sit comfortably on a chair or floor with your hands on your lap. Close your eyes and take three deep breathes. Now close your right nostril with your right-hand thumb and inhale deeply through your left nostril. Next close your left nostril with your middle finger and hold for 4 seconds. Then release your thumb and exhale from your right nostril. Wait for 4 seconds and then inhale from the right nostril. Close both nostrils for four seconds and then exhale from your left nostril by releasing your middle finger. Repeat this process for 3-4 minutes. Once done, sit quietly for a few minutes, focusing on your breathing. Notice as you breathe in your body is filled with oxygen or life, and when you breathe out, your body is empty and light. When breathing out, feel that you are releasing all toxins and stress. Once you are done, it's the end of today's session.

I hope you are feeling more relaxed and excited about the future. Your journey has just begun.

Action Step for Today

Your action step for today is that whenever you remember, take three full deep breathes while being present. Do it as many times as you can throughout the day.

Day 2
Benefits of Meditation

"Practice meditation. You will find that you are carrying within your heart a portable paradise."

- **Paramhansa Yogananda**

Whether your goal is to attain enlightenment or just to increase your performance, meditation is a powerful tool to assist with both. Whether you seek the stillness of a monk's mind or to be resilient like a warrior or a bit of both, meditation can help you build an unshakable mindset. Literature has lots of claimed benefits of meditation, but in this chapter, I will only talk about the ones that are scientifically proven. One of the instant and highly studied benefits of meditation is that it helps combat stress. In today's artificial world where even our food is not 100% natural, our body and mind continuously experience stress and deplete over time. According to research, 90 % of doctor visits are stress-related. Meditation can also help you look 10-15 years younger by combating stress and reducing the symptoms of premature aging.

When our mind experiences stress, Inflammatory chemicals called cytokines, are released in response, which can affect our mood, leading to various mental health problems such as depression. Several studies suggest that meditation may reduce depression by decreasing these inflammatory chemicals.

Meditation reduces stress, which helps your body to relax comfortably; therefore, you will experience better sleep. A good night's sleep is critical for your body and mind to recharge and perform. As an entrepreneur, I have always been about hustle. Due to a busy lifestyle, I found it hard to turn off my mind at bedtime. After I started meditation, I could fall asleep within one minute of lying on the bed. While before meditation, I would sleep 8-9 hours and still wake up tired. After I started practicing meditation, I only sleep 6-7 hours and feel recharged and full of energy when I wake up.

Scientists have now discovered the 'neuroplastic' nature of the human brain, which means that our intelligence is not set at birth – and we can enhance and increase the capacity of our brains in ways once believed to be impossible. When our body is in 'flight or fight mode,' our brain capacity significantly decreases. Scientists have found that meditation can help Increase our attention span and learning abilities.

As most of us may be aware that our brain is made up of two halves; left and right. The left side is responsible for logic, reasoning, decision making, and cognitive skills, whereas the right side enables creative thinking and new ideas. The majority of us are only good at using one part of our brains, while some of the top performers have the skill to jump between the left and right side of the brain and use them both effectively as and when required. Researchers have found that meditators have a thicker corpus callosum. Corpus Callosum is a part of our brain which joins the left and right side and facilitates communication between them. People who have thicker corpus callosum can use their brains more effectively by using both parts of their brains simultaneously. While they can perform risk analysis and critical thinking to identify a problem using the left side of their brain, they simultaneously come up with creative ideas to solve this problem by using the right side. A better connection between two sides of the brain comes with great benefits such as better focus, super creativity, and enhanced memory.

Meditation Day 2
Observing your thoughts

The number one reason why most people fail to meditate is that they have this idea that to be a better meditator, you must become thoughtless. It's like sending a 4-year child for a doctorate in university. It just does not work that way. And you do not have to be thoughtless to get many of the benefits from meditation discussed today. Just being on the journey is enough to bring significant shifts in your life. We will discuss more on this in tomorrow's chapter. For now, let's practice what I believe is one of the best ways to meditate for beginners. To be a better meditator, you have to be an observer of your own life. Have you ever noticed that we find a problem very stressful when we are dealing with it, but we can give excellent advice if another person is dealing with the same problem and we are just observing?

By being an observer, I do not mean stop taking actions, far from it. I mean, focus all your energy on the effort and not on the results. Instead, just observe the results and emotions. Be grateful for the good or bad. Learn from them and move on.

So, let's begin today's session. I want you to close your eyes, take three deep breathes, and observe any thoughts you may have. Don't get carried away with them; just watch your mind and its thoughts. If you get carried away, just say cancel and start being an observer again. Let's do this for 5 minutes.

Great. Excellent and Well done. Be proud of what you are doing, as to be good at anything you need to set an intention and take action. You have set an intention by buying this book and taking action by going through the daily chapters. A massive well done. I promise you that you will notice remarkable changes in your body and mind as you progress through this book.

Action Step for Today

Action step for today is to observe your thoughts anytime when you are alone or not doing anything.

Why do Most People fail to Meditate?

"Meditation is not a way of making your mind quiet. It is a way of entering into the quiet that is already there - buried under the 50,000 thoughts the average person thinks every day."

- Deepak Chopra

One of the biggest myths about meditation is that you need to get rid of your thoughts. Let me do an experiment with you.

I give you the next 30 seconds to close your eyes and think of a white polar bear.

Once you have done this, I want you to close your eyes again for 30 seconds and think of anything you want as long as it's not the white polar bear. You are free to think anything but the polar bear. OK go.

So did you think about the polar bear at least once or maybe more times. If you are like me and many others who have done this experiment, your answer would be yes. The point is our mind and thoughts behave in a way that the more you try to control it, the difficult it gets. The mind, by its very nature, is designed to think and, therefore, will continue to think. You have to let it free and just observe.

Have you ever noticed that you can keep performing your tasks while the mind is busy thinking? This is because, when you are thinking, only 1% of the brain is potentially involved in this thinking process. And so, if you are sitting doing nothing else, 99% of your brain is silent, even when there are thoughts in your mind. It's because this 1% of your brain creates the noise, the remaining 99% gets drawn to it. Hopefully, when you get this concept in your mind, you will be able to take your focus off from that 1% without resisting and just observing.

One of the other main reasons why people do not meditate is that they are too busy? You need to realize that our brains are designed to assist us in our survival, and would naturally resist anytime we want to try something new. The reality is as meditation increases our body and mind performance, we become more productive and hence create more time. Gandhi was once found quoting that, "today I need to meditate for two hours instead of one as I need to get a lot more done." So, please stop telling yourself that you do not have 10 minutes in

24 hours for meditation. All it takes is 10 minutes a day to notice a profound impact on your body and mind, and once you start seeing these changes, you can increase the time you meditate to 20 minutes or half an hour. I meditate only 20 minutes every day. Ten minutes in the morning soon after I wake up and 10 minutes before I go to bed.

Some people start meditating and then give up after a few days thinking that it's not for them. They complain that they are not getting results or things are getting worse. Now the way meditation works is that it starts by making you more aware, in the moment. This means that you will have increased focus, more creativity, and better problem-solving skills. But it also means that as you become aware, you start noticing problems quickly. And all you need to do is fix them if you can and let them be if you can't. Don't give it too much attention. It's better if you are aware of the problem, cause when your mind is too busy, you do not live in the moment and hence do not notice any problems until they become major.

It is crucial to understand that meditation does not change your life; it changes your mind, body, and spirit. As a result, the way you approach life changes, and hence your life changes. Therefore, you cannot expect immediate results. You will notice some instant stress relief and better sleep, but performance-related results will start showing up after a while, maybe in one to three months.

Meditation Day 3
Body Scan: Mindfulness meditation

Sit comfortably on a chair or the floor. Close your eyes and take three long, deep breaths. Feel the rising and falling sensation in your body as you breathe in and out. Now take your attention to the top of your skull, feel the weight of your hair. Slowly bring your attention to your forehead and then your face. Listen to any sounds you can hear, try, and separate the sounds by giving attention to different sources of sounds. Breathe and smell the air. Notice the temperature of the air as you breathe in. Next, take your focus down to your neck and throat. Move your head from left to right and right to left while feeling any stretch in your neck muscles. Now move your attention to your shoulders, then your hands and fingertips. Feel if there is any stiffness or if your muscles are relaxed. Now lift your shoulders, so they touch your ears and then relax as you drop them loose. Next, bring your palms to close together, so they are facing each other but are about 5-10 cm apart. Feel the air between your palms. Then relax your hands on your lap again. Take your attention to the center of your heart. Feel how your lungs expand and contract as you breathe in and out.

Notice any discomfort in your back muscles. Slowly twist to the left side. Place the right hand on the outside of the left knee and place the left hand behind the back to provide support. Take three deep breathes, then return to center. Repeat on the other side. Now take your attention to the lower back, abdominal area, and then the hips. Feel the ground or the chair supporting your weight. Now slowly bring your focus down to your thighs, knees, calves, and then the feet. Notice if your muscles are relaxed or stiff. Wiggle your toes. Now bring your attention back to the root of your backbone. Slowly take your awareness up through your spine, then to your neck and the top of your skull. Be here for 2 minutes, noticing any sensations in your body.

Awesome. Congratulations to you for completing Day 3 of this challenge. It requires a commitment to act on your intentions.

Action Step for Today

The action step for today is to breathe with intention. Try changing the pace of your breathing several times during the day. Every time you touch your phone today, take a full deep breath before unlocking it.

Day 4
How to Stay Present?

"Realize deeply that the present moment is all you have. Make the NOW the primary focus of your life."

- **Eckhart Tolle**

I often get asked that 'How does one stay in the NOW?'. This question itself is incorrect. You can only stay in the NOW. I do not know a single person who can stay in the past or future. The problem arises when we 'try' to stay in the now. We make staying in the now, an act of doing. As if we need to do something to be in the now. The truth, however, is that you do not need to do anything to be present or stay in the moment. You just have to realize that there is no other place you can be but in the NOW.

Whenever we are thinking about the past, we are reliving the past in the now. Hence, we are creating multiple copies of the same now in our minds. A now that happened in the past and thought in the present about the same past. If we are thinking about the future, we are considering all that could happen in our lives, mostly negatives. Hence, damaging the now by destroying our state of mind. Nothing can ever be changed in the past, and nothing can ever be created in the future. All the changes and creations happen in the NOW. The only way we can change our Past and affect our Future is by being in the Present.

Past and Future in real terms are only thoughts in our heads. The reality and action only happen in the now, the present. Another question which I get asked a lot is, "How can one stop thinking about past and present?". Let me ask you something, "When do you think about past and present?" Is it when you are having the best times of your life? When you are living your dream? Or, when you are having a tough time? It is often the latter. So one way to turn this around is by looking at the brighter side, focussing on the often ignored good things which are happening in life.

I am not suggesting that you ignore things that cause you pain or unhappiness. All I am suggesting is that you stop ignoring things that are good in your life. 90% of the stuff in our life is usually the way we want them to be, yet we give 100% attention to the 10% things which are not as per our liking.

Another question which I get asked is that, 'if I stopped thinking about past and present, how will I learn the lessons from past, and plan for my future?' There is nothing wrong with consciously thinking about past or future when needed. The problem arises when we unconsciously drift in the past or future and start living life like zombies on autopilot.

We have become accustomed to the modern lifestyle where multitasking is overrated and thinking something, doing something has become a lifestyle. Therefore rewiring our brain to be fully present will require constant practice. You can bring your awareness in the present by just asking certain questions to yourself at several points during the day, such as – What am I thinking? What am I doing? What can I smell? What different noises can I hear at this moment? Remember, if you are not in the NOW, you are on autopilot. You are not living; you are sleeping. It's time to wake up.

Meditation Day 4
Meditation for Being in Now

Lie down on a mat or floor, on your back. Put your right hand on your belly. Start taking deep breaths. When you inhale, feel how the air is filling your body, and your stomach is expanding. When you exhale, relax your body and feel how the belly goes down, and the body sinks into the floor completely relaxed. Scan your body from head to toe. Rest your attention for a few seconds on areas where you feel stiffness or discomfort before moving on. Lie there for few minutes listening to any sounds, and feeling the support of the floor under you. Try and be present in your body and keep observing any feelings of sensations.

Action Steps for Today

We run on autopilot all day. Doing something and thinking about something else. For today observe the things you do on autopilot like driving brushing your teeth etc. Feel the floor supporting you. Observe your hand motion. Notice the temperature in the room, listen to all the noises around you.

Smell the air. Brush your teeth using the left-hand today, or if you are left-handed, brush your teeth using right-hand today.

Chakra System

"The body is the vehicle, consciousness the driver. Yoga is the path, and the chakras are the map."

- **Anodea Judith**

One of the earliest references to Chakras or energy centers in the human body comes from Vedas and Upanishads (ancient religious texts written in India). According to these scriptures, there are seven chakras in the human body. These chakras support the proper function of our body and mind. Kundalini also referred to as 'life force' or the 'primordial energy,' enters the human body from the top of the skull, giving life to the body and activating all seven chakras when a child is three and a half months old in the mother's womb. This energy then rests into the sacrum bone, a triangular-shaped bone at the bottom of our spine. The word sacrum comes from a Latin phrase, which means sacred. There are some schools of thought that believe that the bone got its name because the kundalini resides in it.

Ancient yogic literature suggests that the prime purpose of human life is for humans to awaken their kundalini and establish a connection with the all-pervading life force. It is believed that once this is achieved, a person can access the states of higher consciousness and superhuman qualities. Some schools of thought also believe that since all matter is made up of energy, a person who has awakened their kundalini can perform miracles in the material world. They can do so as they have established a connection with the all-pervading energy source, also known as prana or chi.

There have been various incidents reported where people have cured incurable diseases through energy healing. Once a person's kundalini is awakened, it also recharges all chakras. Hence, chakras start functioning the way they should be, and any diagnosed or undiagnosed health issues are resolved. The seven chakras in our body are located on the central nervous system, also referred to as Sushumna Nadi, in ancient texts. We also have Ida and Pingala Nadis, which are referred to as the parasympathetic and sympathetic nervous system.

Ida Nadi runs down the left side of the spinal cord and impacts the right side of the brain. An Ida dominant person will be creative and intuitive. However, over dominance of Ida Nadi may lead to a person being overly emotional and sometimes lazy. Such a person may find that they have lots of ideas but somehow fail to execute them. Ida dominant people also tend to overthink about the past. Pingala Nadi runs down the right side of the spine and impacts the left side of the brain.

A Pingala dominant person is good at solving problems and taking actions. However, over dominance of this Nadi may lead to increased stress and excessive planning. Pingala dominant people tend to think more about the future. To harness the power and qualities of both Nadis one must practice being present and balanced.

Meditation Day 5
Chakra Meditation

Sit comfortably on the floor or a chair with your spine erect but not stressed. You can support your back, but keep your head free. Take your attention above your head up through your ceiling into the sky past the stars and planets. You will notice that once you take your attention high enough, you get to a place where there is nothing, a void space. Imagine a stream of white light coming down from this place into the top of the crown. Imagine the light going into your head, face, neck shoulders, down your arms. Feel the light filling your lungs, heart, abdomen, then going down your hips, thighs, legs, and feet. Now take your attention to the bottom of your spine where the root chakra is located. Imagine a red color light radiating around from your root chakra. Now slowly take your attention up your spine to the sacral chakra. This is located on your spine between your navel and root chakra. Visualize an orange color light radiating from this chakra. Take a deep breath in and slowly take your attention further up your spine to the area where your navel point is. This is the place for solar plexus chakra. Visualize your solar plexus chakra on your spine in the form of bright yellow light. Next, take your attention to the center of your chest. This is the place of the heart chakra. Imagine the heart chakra radiating a bright green light. Slowly take your attention to your throat chakra. Visualize this chakra shining a solid blue light. Now moving your attention up the spine, take it to the area between your eyebrows on your forehead. Visualize your third eye chakra radiating an indigo colored light. Slowly push your attention up and around your crown area. Imagine your crown area shining a bright violet light. Visualize your kundalini rising up slowly in the form of white light from the root of your spine, energizing all chakras, and then coming out from your crown to meet the all-pervading energy which is everywhere around us. Meditate in this state for 2 minutes.

Congratulations on completing the Day 5 of this program. I can bet you would have started noticing small changes in your day to day life, whether it is a shift towards positive thinking, a sense of calmness, or increased productivity. Please record any new experience in your meditation journal and feel free to share it with all of us on the Facebook group.

Action Step for Today

Most of us tend to be Ida or Pingala dominant at different times of the day. Try and observe your behavior to notice which side you are leaning towards. Bring yourself back to the balance by taking three deep breaths whenever you find yourself overthinking.

Day 6
Three values for evolving your consciousness

If you want to raise your consciousness, you must focus on adapting three core values – Compassion, Forgiveness, and Gratitude. This chapter will discuss Compassion. Forgiveness and Gratitude will be covered in the following chapters.

Compassion

"If you want others to be happy, practice compassion. If you want to be happy, practice compassion."

- **The Dalai Lama**

Dr Hawkins, a well-known spiritual teacher, and psychiatrist, developed a Map of Consciousness. The map shows the vibrational energy of different emotional states. In the map, Love has an energy frequency of 500. This is also shown as the energy frequency above which we enter the 5th Dimension of consciousness. This implies that in order to access the states of higher consciousness, you must be in the energy frequency of love and above.

According to another research done by Richard J Davidson, compassion is a trainable skill. People who practice compassion have a more positive outlook on life and are less likely to be stressed. It was also found that people who practice self-compassion could slow the process of aging. Practicing compassion can also enhance your emotional intelligence skills. Emotional intelligence is hugely beneficial for building relations and coping with the challenges of life in general.

The Power of Self-Compassion – *Why You Must Love You?*

Do you remember the time when you first started walking (maybe you don't – but you get the zest), everyone around was so encouraging, some even clapped and even when you fell you heard phrases like, "brave boy/girl," "well done," "try again" etc. And you tried, again, and again till you got it. Even little things like holding a spoon and drawing a straight line were celebrated. Fast forward a few decades later, you run companies, manage families, get up and try every day, but who is celebrating for all you do? Who is encouraging? Do you ever hear words like 'try again,' 'brave boy/girl,' etc.? Half of the time, no one, but only you know how hard you are trying or what you have been through. Self-compassion, therefore, becomes your duty to yourself. Appreciate what you have done, what you are doing, and ignore the small mistakes you make along the way, as we are all just learning 'to live.'

You may have learned in people management courses on how to avoid negative feedback for staff motivation. How about we stop giving negative feedback to ourselves for our motivation? Self-compassion brings an immediate feeling of peace and happiness. Think about it this way, if you had a friend who you could not get rid of, but the person is constantly nagging and trying to find problems in you. What effect will this person have on you? Now think what you are doing to yourself when you are self-criticizing. According to Marisa Peer (one of UK's famous mental health coach), 'the most effective way to boost your self-esteem is self-praise'. Marisa has coached many successful millionaires and billionaires, and one of the healing exercises Marisa asks her mentees to do is to write a simple note on their mirror, which reads – 'I AM ENOUGH.' This simple note has brought drastic changes to the life of many individuals, which just shows the power of self-compassion.

Below are a few ways you can practice self-compassion:

> **Pay Attention to your self-talk:** Notice how you talk to yourself, particularly at stressful times or after making a mistake. Instead of saying 'I am so stupid' chose to say, 'I made a mistake, but its OK and I am learning.'

- ➢ **Appreciate and Praise yourself often:** Now, I know that we live in a society where modesty is considered admirable. However, when you are talking to yourself, no one else is listening. So, next time you do something nice, I give you the freedom to praise yourself, clap for yourself, and celebrate your smallest achievements.
- ➢ **Practice Gratitude:** Every morning and just before going to bed, list at least five things that are good about you and be grateful for them.

Remember, everyone you know will play a long or short role in your life, but the person you see in the mirror will live it all with you. So be nice.

Meditation Day 6
Compassion Meditation

Sit comfortably on a chair or floor. Keep your back supported and head free. Keep your left hand on your lap and right hand on your heart. Now think of a person who you love unconditionally, it could be a person or a pet. Feel your love for this person in your heart. Now slowly take your full attention only on this feeling. Visualize this feeling as a red light in your heart. Slowly bring your right hand off your heart and rest it on your lap. Now feel the red light in your heart (which represents pure compassion) expanding and filling your whole body—slowly filling your chest, your neck, your face, your shoulders, your hands, your abdomen, your thighs, your legs, and your feet. Feel this compassion for you. You work hard every day, and you deserve your kindness more than anyone else. So take the time to fill yourself first.

Once you have meditated in this state for a minute, imagine this red light expanding outside your body, filling the room you are in, the town you are in, the state you are in, the country you are in, and slowly filling the planet. Feel giving out the energy of compassion to everything and everyone in the world. Meditate in this state for a minute.

Now imagine receiving the same compassion back from everything and everyone in the world. Visualize this as the red light coming back to you, filling you with even more compassion and love. Stretch your arms out to receive this compassion. Meditate in this state for a minute.

Congratulations on finishing the Day 6. People around you might have started to notice the change in your energy frequency now.

Action Steps for Today

1. Make one nice gesture to yourself. It could be taking half an hour out to get a bath without worrying about time, getting a massage, or buying a cup of coffee for yourself. Note that you are making this gesture to you as you believe that you deserve it. The most important part of this exercise is that you should enjoy whatever it is without worrying about time and guilt-free.
2. Make one nice gesture to someone you do not know and will never meet again. It could be giving some money to the homeless, buying a stranger a cup of coffee, or just smiling at every person you see. Feel your compassion towards this person while you are making the gesture.

Forgiveness

"Holding on to anger is like grasping a hot coal with the intent of throwing it at someone else: you are the one who gets burned."

- Buddha

The quicker you FORGIVE, the happier you will LIVE

In his book Forgive for Good: A Proven Prescription for Health and Happiness, Fred Luskin writes that forgiveness is "taking back your power," "about your healing," and is "for you and not the offender."

So, what exactly is forgiveness? Forgiveness sets you free. It could be defined as giving up my right to hurt you for hurting me. It means I do not have to hear you say 'I am sorry' for me to move forward with my life. The purpose of forgiveness is to set the victim free. It has nothing to do with the offender.

Anne Lamott defines it the best in her quote - "Not forgiving is like drinking rat poison and then waiting for the rat to die." When we do not forgive someone, it is we who suffer as we are tied to the chains of the negative experience, which always reminds us about it. Isabelle Holland explains this further - "As long as you don't forgive, who and whatever it is will occupy a rent-free space in your mind."

But **why Forgive?** Forgiving could be extremely difficult, and some may even feel that forgiving someone may not be the fair or the right thing to do. After all, the person who has given us pain must suffer and realize that they were wrong. Although the real truth is that when we don't forgive someone, we are punishing us and not the person who we are not forgiving. That person may not even realize and not even care about whether we forgive them or not. Every grudge we hold in our brain acts as fog and damages our mental health and wellbeing. The pain we are causing to our brain by holding this grudge is often multiple times more than the actual pain that was inflicted by this person.

When we don't forgive someone, we are continually using a part of our energy to fight this person in our subconscious mind. Imagine if you do not forgive a person for ten years how much energy you are wasting. Now times this by 2, 3 or more depending on how many people you are not forgiving. All this wasted energy could be used for your growth. When you forgive someone, you are setting yourself free from them and them from you. **You are not acknowledging that what they did to you was OK**. But what you are doing is saying that you are free from them and they are from you as there is nothing you need from them. You can heal you by yourself and do not need their apology or suffering.

Scientists have noted that forgiving can significantly spike the alpha waves in both hemispheres of the brain. Alpha waves are responsible for our intuition, creativity, and learning new skills. The question, therefore, is not why forgive? But why won't we forgive?

We have already discussed that it's not easy to forgive. Many argue that it can be the most challenging thing to do. Although the truth is, it is not difficult at all. As a child, we all were excellent forgivers. Have you ever noticed a child holding a grudge against someone? A child can get annoyed by you, and the very next moment can be hugging and kissing you. This comes naturally to them. The reason why we find forgiving difficult is that as we grow up, our personalities take over our conscious (or real) self. Our characters are developed by our families, societies, and education.

As we grow, we are taught what is wrong and what is right. We hear stories and watch movies about how the evil or the wronged is always punished at the end. We, therefore, build an expectation that the person who has done wrong to us must realize their mistake and feel sorry. However, in reality, things don't work this way. In the real-world, while you are busy thinking that someone must feel sorry for what they did, the other person may be thinking you must feel sorry for what you did. So, you both end up punishing yourself for what you did not do. You did not forgive. If there is one thing you can teach your child, teach them that 'it is more important to be happy than to prove yourself right or the other person wrong.' You are only responsible for your happiness. You are not responsible for teaching others a lesson.

How to Forgive? Before we get to the process of forgiveness, let's make it clear What forgiveness is and is not:

WHAT FORGIVENESS IS <u>NOT</u>

➢ Forgiveness is not – an act of giving to the offender.
➢ Forgiveness does not – require one person to apologize or feel sorry.
➢ Forgiveness does not – pardon the person of their wrongdoings.
➢ Forgiveness does not – mean admitting what was done or what happened was OK.

WHAT FORGIVENESS <u>IS</u>

➢ Forgiveness is – a healing gift that you give to yourselves.
➢ Forgiveness is – freeing up yourself from your past.
➢ Forgiveness is – claiming back your happiness and realizing that you cannot let one single event or incident from the past dictate your life.
➢ Forgiveness is – getting rid of the poison from our system.

Let's explain this last point with an example. Suppose a snake bites you. What do you do next? You have two choices. One option is to run around finding that snake and beat it till it feels sorry. But what happens while you are doing this is that the poison is spreading inside you. The other option is to forget about the snake and get rid of the poison first. Forgiveness is taking care of yourself. Do it for yourself.

<u>Four Steps for Forgiveness:</u>

1. **Increase the blood circulation in Your Brain**. Do a short breathing exercise or meditation to get the blood supply to the prefrontal cortex, a part of the brain

responsible for logical thinking, empathy, and forgiveness.

2. **Reframe the experience**. Realize that whatever has happened is nothing about you and everything about the person who did it. It could be because they have grown up in a certain way. They have suffered previously, which has changed their personality. There could be a lot of reasons for people to behave in a certain way. There are two quotes that I find helpful. One is 'Hurt people hurt people,' and the other is 'NO child is born evil.' Remember, we are not justifying what they did was wrong. We are only making assumptions to help our brain in the process of forgiveness.

3. **Take responsibility** for your feelings. What happened to you has nothing to do with you and is all about the person who did it. But how you feel, as a result, is your responsibility. Responsibility is the ability to respond. Whatever they did to you is depended on their level of thinking and mindset. However, your happiness is your responsibility. Do not let your feelings be dictated by other people's actions.

4. **Recreate your story.** Recreate your own Hero story. Where you have an Unshakable resilience to deal with the most challenging situations life can throw at you. Think about these people or incidents as a nudge by Universe to hint you that it's time to grow. I like the quote from the movie 'My Giant' – 'Without Goliath, David is just a punk kid throwing rocks.' Whatever wrong has happened in your life is what illuminates the greatness of the Hero you are.

Make Forgiveness a daily ritual. Forgive everything and everyone before you go to bed each night. You will feel much lighter and live much happier.

Meditation Day 7
Forgiveness Meditation

Before we begin today's meditation, I want to ask you to have faith and do all the steps. Remember that everything you are doing is only for you to know and in your mind. It's for your healing. If you are not comfortable yet to forgive someone, you can skip that section or forgive another person who you feel comfortable forgiving. However, you will only get the full benefits from this practice once you forgive everyone.

When you are ready, find a comfortable place to either sit or lie down. If you are sitting, sit with your back supported and head free. Take a few deep breaths. Now gently grab the back of your head with your right hand. Tilt your head slightly up, so that it is pushing into our palm. Think of a time when you felt guilty for doing something. If any feelings of discomfort or any resent come up, focus where this feeling is strong in your body. Now breathe into this place. Visualize a white light flowing in this area as you breathe in, dissolving any trapped resent or guilt. As you breathe out, feel that you are releasing this trapped energy. Now repeat three times – "I forgive myself for any wrongdoings. What was done is in the past. I am just learning how to live. I love me, and I bless me." Bring your right hand back on your lap, your head straight, and meditate for a minute. Every time you breathe in, feel the energy flowing into you, and when you breathe out, imagine releasing any trapped energy.

Next, gently grab your forehead with your right hand. Think of a time when you felt angry because someone did something.

If any feelings of anger or frustration come up, focus where this feeling is strong in your body. Now breathe into this place. Visualize a white light flowing in this area as you breathe in, dissolving any trapped anger or frustration. As you breathe out, feel that you are releasing this trapped energy. Now imagine this person standing in front of you and repeat three times – "I forgive you for any wrongdoings. What was done is in the past. I understand that you have your problems, and you are learning how to live. I love you, and I bless you." Bring your right hand back on your lap, your head straight, and meditate for a minute. Every time you breathe in, feel the energy flowing into you, and when you breathe out, imagine releasing any trapped energy.

Congratulations on completing Day 7. Most people find today's session the most challenging element of meditation, but you will also see the most significant shift in your energy levels after this session. I would recommend going back to this at least once a week.

Action Step for Today

Observe your reactions to events. Every time you feel frustrated or angry with someone or something, repeat in your mind, "I love you, I bless you."

Day 8
Gratitude

"God gave you a gift of 86,400 seconds today. Have you used one to say thank you."

-William Arthur Ward

If there is one question which undoubtedly the whole human species on the planet will answer 'YES' to is 'Do you want to be happy?'. We are going to start this chapter by discussing – If there is a connection between this universal desire of the human race and gratitude? Some may believe that if you are happy, then you will be grateful, and it seems the apparent connection. But what if I ask you to think carefully if this is true? Is it really that happy people are grateful? We all know someone who has everything one could ask for to be happy and they still are miserable. They are always seeking for something. At times they are not even sure what they are seeking. Then there are also people who have all the misfortune one can have but still radiate happiness. Why? It's because they are grateful for whatever they have. It is not happiness which makes you grateful, but gratefulness which will make you happy.

Gratitude has become the most talked about things in the personal growth world in recent years. In the last decade, several studies have supported the effectiveness of practicing daily gratitude. Studies show that people who practice gratitude as a daily ritual are generally more positive, happier, and healthier. Research has shown that Practicing gratitude can lower the levels of cortisol, a stress-causing hormone, and can boost performance and productivity. Some studies also indicate that people who practice gratefulness, generally sleep better, and express more compassion and kindness.

Gratitude helps you shift your vision. By the law of attraction, we attract what we focus on. If we continuously focus on things which we are grateful for, what are we more likely to attract? – More things to be grateful for.

But how to practice gratitude? There are two things which you need to experience Gratitude. Something valuable must be given to you. And the value of this something must be far higher than the efforts (if any) you had to put to receive it. What is the one thing which we all are given at any time without making much effort to earn it? It is the present moment. Every present moment is an opportunity which is given to us. We can do anything with that moment, and if we did not use it the way we intended, we are given another moment and then another. Start your gratitude practice by being grateful for the present moment. This will also shift your perspective as you will start looking at every present moment as an opportunity.

As a species, our brains have been wired to help us survive; therefore, we automatically and constantly notice what is broken, undone, or lacking in our lives. How can we rewire our brain so we can experience all these fantastic benefits of Gratitude? Gandhi once said, "I cried because I had no shoes, then I met a man who had no feet." Gratitude is about counting your blessings. We do not need to look for reasons to be grateful. If you are reading this, chances are you have too many reasons already. If you wake up healthy, you are already living someone's dream.

Here are a few techniques you can use to make gratitude a part of your day to day life:

➤ Start a Gratitude journal. Every day note down 5-10 things you are grateful for in your life. It could be as simple as having a roof above your head to maybe some recent achievement or event. Sometimes you can even use the power of gratitude to manifest things you don't yet have. You can say something like I am grateful that more and more money is coming to me, or I am thankful that my dream job will be mine soon. This will put you in the right energy frequency to receive these things. Make this activity a part of your morning or bedtime ritual.

➤ Make a Gratitude board or collage and stick it on your wall, put it on Pinterest, or make it your desktop cover. Whenever you see it, you will be reminded of your commitment to living gratefully.

> Accept the challenge of finding the hidden blessing in every setback. Example: Stuck in traffic? Use the time to meditate (with your eyes open, of course – just focus on your breathing) or listen to an audiobook, then take this as a learning experience of how to deal with an annoyed boss or how to manage your time effectively to leave work early next day. Now you can be thankful for this opportunity.

> Whenever you experience a difficult situation, remember this quote from Gandhi: "I cried because I had no shoes, then I met a man who had no feet." Then close your eyes and think of 4-5 things you are grateful for. This will boost neurotransmitter serotonin and activate the brain stem to produce dopamine. You will instantly start feeling better and be in a better state of mind to deal with the situation.

As you practice gratitude, you will notice an inner shift. You will become a happier and more positive person. And as a result, your relationships, productivity, and sleep will all significantly improve over time.

Meditation Day 8
Gratitude Meditation

When you are ready, find a comfortable place to sit or lie down. If you are sitting, have your back supported but head free. Take a few deep breaths. Observe the rising and falling sensation in your body. Be grateful for now. Be grateful for the peace which is within you at this very moment. Now think of three things about you for which you are grateful. It could be that you are healthy, or you are committed to your growth or that you are a good person in general. Feel the feeling of gratefulness in your body, in your heart, in your mind.

Next, think of three material things you are grateful for. It could be the house you live in, the car you drive, the money you have, or just that you have enough food to keep you alive. Finally, think of three non-material things you are grateful for. This could be your child, the sunshine, or just that you have some people in your life who love you and support you.

Every incident, good or bad, every person good or bad, is there in your life to support you or nudge you to grow. So be grateful for everything and everyone. Notice where you feel this feeling. Some people feel this in their gut, others feel it in their heart, and some feel it in their mind. Focus on this feeling and imagine it expanding, bigger than your body, bigger than your house, bigger than your country and bigger than the world. See this as a light radiating from you, sending gratitude to every person on this planet. Now imagine this light or energy reflecting from everyone coming back to you. Observe it. Meditate in this state for a few minutes.

Congratulations on finishing Day 8. Your inner energy is expanding and will soon begin changing the world around you.

Action Steps for Today

Practice being grateful for other people. When you see a nice car, be grateful for the person who owns it. When you see a happy family, be grateful for them. When you see someone healthy and strong, be grateful for their health and strength.

Mindfulness: doing things consciously

"Because you are alive, everything is possible."

-    Thich Nhat Hanh

Over the next few chapters, we will discuss some of the most practiced and talked about techniques of Meditation. In this chapter, I will talk about Mindfulness.

The mindfulness meditation technique is derived from Vipassana, which is one of the oldest forms of meditation practice in Buddhism. The word Vipassana means 'insight' – **an awareness of things as they happen**. This is also the fundamental principle behind Mindfulness. It is essential to understand and adopt this principle in your life to benefit from mindfulness or Vipassana technique.

There are two kinds of meditative practices taught in Buddhism – Vipassana and Samatha. The meaning of Samatha is 'Tranquility' – A state of mind where there are no thoughts and the mind is at rest. Vipassana and Samatha can also be understood as two stages of meditation – Awareness and Thoughtless awareness. I will talk more about Thoughtless Awareness on day 14. Most of the meditation practices follow the principles of Samatha, where they try to train the mind to focus on a particular object or mantra and get rid of any other thoughts. Mindfulness encourages individuals to be mindful of their thoughts instead of trying to control them. You watch your thoughts as they come and go without judgment.

What is mindfulness?

There is a lot of buzz these days about Mindfulness and its proven benefits. The research has shown that practicing mindfulness will lower stress levels and chances of depression, and increase focus and happiness. But what exactly is Mindfulness and how to Practice it? In short – it is a practice to develop one's ability to be fully present in the moment. In this chapter, I will discuss everything you need to know to get started.

Being mindful means being fully aware of the present moment and putting all your attention in the here and now. It involves observing your thoughts without labeling them good or bad. The ultimate goal is to be in the state as we go through the ups and downs of our daily life.

Multitasking is overrated. You cannot be more productive by doing three things at once. The reason why children are excellent learners is that they are totally present. In today's world, we are so full of distractions that as we grow up, distraction becomes our addiction. If we don't have distractions around us, we start feeling uncomfortable or 'bored.' This is the reason why to integrate mindfulness in your daily life; you will need to set aside 10-20 minutes every day to practice mindfulness consciously. This will train your brain to be present and live in the moment.

Have you ever regretted your action or decision after it has happened? The problem is that most of us live on autopilot. Most of the choices we make and the way we react is based on past experiences or downloads we have had in our brains from our families and society. We fail to consider that every situation is different, and we can choose our reaction or decision consciously without any references from the past. Research shows that an average person spends about 50% of their time thinking about the past or present. This means we can double our productivity just by being in the present moment.

How is Mindfulness different from other meditation techniques?

Mindfulness is more than a meditation practice. It is a way of living. Once you understand this, practicing mindfulness becomes very easy and is an excellent way to meditate for beginners as it does not require much effort or time. You can practice mindfulness while performing any of your daily activities. Walking to work? Use all your senses to live the walk. Focus on your breathing - do you notice any smell around? Listen to the sounds – is there any sound that stands out? Can you hear the sounds coming from far away? Look around – What do you see? Is there anything you haven't noticed before? How is the temperature of the air? – Cold/Warm. Are you holding something? – Feel its texture, weight, pattern

By practicing mindfulness meditation regularly, we train our minds for short durations. As the mind becomes more familiar with the process, living in the present comes naturally to us. A common misconception is that mindfulness helps to get rid of your emotions. The reality is far from it. As you are more present, you will experience the emotions even more strongly. But because you are present, you will not react to these emotions on autopilot. You would acknowledge the feelings and chose your response. Research shows that practicing mindfulness can increase grey matter – the part of the brain responsible for managing emotions and problem-solving.

Meditation Day 9
Mindfulness Practice

Sit comfortably on a chair or floor with your back supported and head free. Close your eyes and take a few deep breaths. Bring your attention in the now. Notice any sensations in the body. Do you notice any stiffness or discomfort? Send some energy to this part of the body. Now slowly expand your awareness outside your body. Without opening your eyes, try and feel what is around you? Feel the floor supporting you; feel the temperature in the room. Feel your presence in the room. Can you hear any sounds, from nearby or far away? Try and differentiate the sounds if you hear more than one. Now bring your attention to your breath. Meditate here for few minutes. Every time your mind wanders off, gently bring it back to your breath, without any judgment.

Congratulations on completing Day 9. You are doing amazing.

Action Step for Today

A great mindfulness practice was taught to us as a kid when we were learning to cross the street. Stop, look around and Go. Make this as a daily ritual to do it as many times as it occurs. Stop Look Go.

Power of mantras - Mantra or Affirmations

"A mantra is .... a collection of words strung together to create a positive effect."

- **Robin Sharma**

We often hear about mantras, and the word is used quite a bit whenever one talks about meditation or spiritual growth. However, most people consider it to be too hokey or esoteric. Many also believe that mantras are only attached to specific religious or spiritual practices and are not for everyone to use, although science takes a fascinating view of this. The word 'mantra' is derived from two Sanskrit words: 'man' meaning mind and 'tra' meaning tool. Hence it could be concluded that in ancient times mantras were used as a 'tool for the mind.' Studies have confirmed that mantras have the power to reprogram our brains to think more positively. They can act as an anchor to keep your attention on things or values you want to focus on.

The Neurological Effects of Mantra

While science has just started to catch up on the benefits of reciting mantra on our brain, yogis from the eastern world have been using mantras as a powerful meditation tool since more than 3000 years ago. Studies that monitored brain activity through advanced brain imaging tools confirm that the practice of chanting mantras could be extremely beneficial to clear our mind from background chatter and calm our nervous system.

In a study published in the Journal of Cognitive Enhancement, Researcher's from a Swedish University performed an experiment to determine the effects of practicing mantra meditation on the human brain. They measured activity in an area of the brain called the default mode network (a part that becomes active when we do self-reflection or aimless thinking). Medical science suggests that an overactive default mode network can imply that the person will feel distracted and restless.

In the experiment, a group of participants was asked to practice two weeks of kundalini yoga. Each session included some yoga exercises followed by 11 minutes of mantra meditation. The study found that practicing mantra meditation can significantly suppress activity in the default mode network. Research also indicates that you do not have to chant Sanskrit rhymes to get benefits of mantra meditation. As long as you repeat any word or phrase and focus your attention on this sound, you can get the benefits.

How to Practice Mantras

Mantras are used in transcendental meditation techniques. This technique is particularly useful to attain a stage of relaxed awareness. It involves repeating a mantra several times with your eyes closed. The sound of the mantra is used as an anchor to pull your attention back within you whenever your mind starts to wander. It is a beneficial technique for beginners, as you are learning to calm your mind. One of the most common and ancient mantras used for such meditation is 'om.' In Vedic literature, 'om' or 'a-u-m' has been associated with the 'sound of the Universe' or 'cosmic sound.'

It does not matter which word you use as your mantra. Repetition, consistency, and discipline are more important. It is, however, advisable that the word you use for your mantra must be easy to pronounce, so you do not put too much attention on trying to pronounce it correctly. When reciting a mantra, you must feel the sound within and around you. By regular practice, the syllables in the mantras combined with the power of your consciousness will act as vibrational energy, to shift your inner state.

Meditation Day 10
Mantra Meditation

Sit comfortably on a chair or floor. Close your eyes and take few deep breaths. Now take another deep breath and as you exhale chant om (a-u-m). You can use any other word if you feel more comfortable with that word, such as 'I am.' Feel the vibrations of the sound within and around you. Meditate on this sound for a few minutes. Every time your mind wanders, use the mantra as an anchor to bring it back.

Congratulations on finishing day 10. You are halfway to completing your 21-day challenge. You have started sending signals to the Universe that you are ready for the next level.

Action Step for Today

Anytime you feel overwhelmed today, find a quiet place, then chant your mantra three times. Notice the difference in your mental state just by performing this short exercise.

Kundalini Yoga

"Anything considered spiritual or metaphysical is generally just the physics that we don't yet understand."

- ### Nassim Haramein

What is Kundalini? As we discussed on Day 5, kundalini, also referred to as 'life force' or the 'primordial energy' enters human body from the top of the skull, giving life to the body and activating all seven chakras when a child is 3.5 months old in the mother's womb. This energy then rests into the sacrum bone (a triangular-shaped bone) at the bottom of our spine. The word sacrum comes from a Latin phrase, which means sacred, and some schools of thought believe that the bone was given its name because the kundalini resides in it. The practice of awakening kundalini is referred to as **Kundalini Yoga.**

As per the Vedic scriptures, once a practitioner awakens their kundalini, they attain connection with pure consciousness and are endowed with enlightenment. The practice is at least over 2000 years old. In ancient India, holy sages, also known as rishis, sought enlightenment by exploring the divine power hidden within our body and mind. The techniques they developed through their practices became kundalini yoga. There are about 20 Upanishads which talk about kundalini yoga. Some of the other yogic practices talked about in the Upanishads are Karma yoga – detachment, Raja yoga – meditation, Bhakti yoga – devotion and Hatha yoga – yogic postures and exercises.

There are numerous benefits of practicing kundalini yoga, but one of the main benefits is that it can supercharge your creativity. Think about it. What is the most creative force we all know? Universe, Nature, or source energy whatever we want to call is the single biggest creator of all time. So, when we establish our connection with this power, our brain has access to limitless creativity. There is a misconception that creativity is only relevant to people who are in specific job roles – like artists or designers. While the truth is that creation is all around us. Every moment we are either creating, destroying, or managing.

The problem is that most of us have lost our creativity at a very young age. So we spend the majority of our lives creating an OK life experience and then put all our energy in trying to manage it. Only to end up feeling exhausted and stressed. Our job as humans is not to manage or destroy. That's what the Universe does. We are here to create and create only. When we try to manage, we start acting in contradiction to nature's law and end up destroying whatever we are trying to manage. Therefore, we should solely focus our energy on creating a better life and surrender to the Universe for the management of it. We will talk more about the power of surrender in a later chapter.

Practicing Kundalini yoga recharges all our chakras and resets our brain so we can become the fearless and curious creators like we once were as a child. When kundalini energy recharges the seven chakras or energy centers, it will also cure and heal any of the diseases or health issues. Our chakras are responsible for the proper functioning of different parts of our body. Therefore, once we heal a chakra, we also heal all the body parts that chakra is responsible for.

Meditation Day 11

Sit comfortably in the lotus position or if you can not sit in a lotus position, sit on a chair with your back supported and head free. Put your left hand on your lap with your thumb pressing against your index finger (this is also known as Gyan/knowledge mudra). Place your right hand where your heart is. Take a few deep breaths. Now repeat with me three times, "I am not my body or my brain. I am pure consciousness." Now place your right hand on your forehead and repeat three times, "I forgive everyone, including myself." Take three long breaths, and as you breathe out, imagine that you are exhaling all the blocks and any trapped negative energy. Now take your right hand to the bottom of the spine (from the front) where the kundalini energy resides. Imagine you are lifting your kundalini as you move your right hand from your root chakra to your crown chakra. Repeat this three times. Now place your right hand on your lap with the right thumb touching your right index finger. Keep your attention about two cm above your crown chakra. Do not worry if you can not focus. It is natural for the mind to wander. Just bring your attention back to the top of your crown chakra, every time you get distracted. Meditate in this position for the next 5 min.

Action Step for Today

Perform this step a few times during the day. Put your right hand on your heart and repeat in your mind, "I am not my body or brain. I am pure consciousness."

Day 12
Creative Visualization

"You can change your brain just by thinking differently."

-Dr. Joe Dispenza

We all have a creative force within us. Creative visualization can be effectively used as part of your meditation practice to help relax, boost your mood, heal your body and mind as well as to manifest your future which we will discuss in more detail on Day 20. Whenever we want to achieve something in our lives, most of us start with hustle, hard work, and put too much focus on using our muscle power to get more and more done. We finally end up feeling exhausted and give up or succeed in one aspect of life but lose in others.

A famous spiritual teacher Esther Hicks once said, "Seventeen seconds of focused, pleasurable visualization is stronger than 2000 hours of working to obtain a goal." Creative visualization helps us tap into the power of our subconscious brain. Most people only do goal setting with a conscious mind. Creative visualization helps to communicate these goals to your subconscious mind. If you are unaware of the power of your subconscious mind, think about this for a minute. How many tasks during the day do you perform on autopilot as in when you are doing something while your mind is busy thinking something else. The thinking mind is the conscious mind, and the mind that helps you perform your daily tasks mostly without errors is your subconscious mind.

Our brain thinks in images. As soon as I say 'a pink elephant,' you immediately create a mental image of a pink elephant. Creative visualization can be used for healing, often referred to as Imagery therapy. There is plenty of research to support that this technique is advantageous. Dr. O Carl Simonton of the Simonton Research Centre found that when using imagery therapy to promote healing, patients went through accelerated recovery from life-threatening diseases like cancer.

Why does Creative visualization work?

Research shows that visualizing an experience activates the same neuro pathways in the brain as when having the experience. Another research-based theory suggests that when we imagine things, our subconscious mind starts believing that these things are happening in reality. This affects our self-image, belief, and confidence—the subconscious mind, which is always running, starts looking for related things and opportunities. Opportunities magically start appearing as if they were never there. The reality, however, is that they were always there, you just were not looking. While all this helps us to gain a basic understanding, some of the mysterious results practitioners of this technique have claimed remains beyond the scope of modern-day science.

How does Creative Visualisation work?

We have discussed the many benefits of using creative visualization techniques let's talk about how it works? A creative visualization is an act of actively visualizing or creating a mental image of an experience you want to live. It could be that you want to be free from a disease you have, or you want a particular lifestyle, or something as small as how you want your day to progress. The key is trying to find that time and discipline to get connected to your subconscious mind and then communicating the message through mental images.

The best time to practice Creative Visualisation would be when you are more relaxed and have access to the alpha states of the mind. This is usually just before we fall asleep, and soon after, we wake up or otherwise just after you have finished your daily meditation. We are so much consumed by the modern lifestyle that we have become 'human doings' rather than 'human beings.' Creative visualization techniques help to focus on what we want to be rather than what we want to do. They work like self-hypnosis to shift your inner beliefs and reprogram your subconscious mind.

Meditation Day 12
Practicing Creative Visualization

Sit comfortably with your back supported and head free. Close your eyes and take a few deep breaths. Now visualize a path in front of you. Start walking to this path. You can see lots of trees around you. Feel the small rocks under your shoes.

As you go further, you start seeing the sand and an ocean. It's a bright sunny day. You can feel the heat of the sun on your skin. Feel the cold air gently touching your skin. As you walk further, you notice something written on the sand. This is your current reality. If you don't like something, just rub it off from the sand. Now write three things which you want to show up in your life in this sand. Then sit here, next to the water, and in the sun for a short meditation. When you are ready, open your eyes.

Congratulations on completing Day 12. Your consciousness is expanding.

Action Steps for Today

Make a vision board, and include everything you want to manifest in your life over the next five years. Put it somewhere you can see every day. Try and keep it as visual as possible – more images, less text.

Day 13

The Five-element
Meditation

"All know that the drop merges into the ocean, but few know that the ocean merges into the drop."

- **Kabir**

Ancient philosophy suggests that everything in nature is made up of five elements: earth, water, fire, air, and space. Incorporating these elements in your mediation practice can bring huge benefits, particularly for clearance and healing of your body and mind. Most methods of yoga are based on these five elements. The five elements also form the basis of Ayurveda, one of the world's oldest medical system originated in traditional India. Therefore, my advice is if you want to go deeper into higher states of meditation, you must use the knowledge of these elements.

The five elements represent different states of matter. Everything which is in solid-state is a representative of Earth, all Liquids are Water, and all gas is Air. Fire is represented by heat and is considered a strong element that can change the state of one element to another. For example, if we heat water, it becomes steam (Air). Fire is used by various yogic and tantric rituals to control and purify the other states of matter. Space is above all the other four states of matter, and it is what is holding everything together. Without space, everything will appear as one/ the ultimate reality. It is due to this that many spiritual teachers have suggested that space is the only reality; everything else is an illusion. According to the latest research, 99.99% of our body is empty space.

Human Body

Each element plays a vital role in the functioning of our body. Earth makes all the solid structures such as bones and the muscles. Liquid components of the body, such as blood or saliva, comprise Water. All movements within the body are facilitated by air. Fire helps in digestion and other bodily functions. And space is what holds it all together and also constitutes the energy field around our body.

A disease occurs whenever there is an imbalance in these elements. By using the right techniques and meditation, it is possible to fix the imbalance and any resulting illness. Fire, air, and water are the most common elements used in yogic practices to clear any blocks from body and mind.

Meditation Day 13
Using the Five Elements for Clearance and Healing

For performing this meditation, you would need a big tub of water. Big enough to put your both feet in it. Ideally, this tub must not be made up of plastic. However, if you do not have anything else available, it is ok to use a plastic tub until you find an alternative. You would also need some sea salt and a candle. Light the candle in front of you but slightly towards the left side of your body. This is because the right side or Pingala Nadi, as discussed on Day 5, can become imbalanced if it's overheated. Now fill your tub with water and put it near a chair where you will sit for your meditation. Mix some warm water to adjust the temperature, so the water is not too cold. Now add some sea salt in it. Adding sea salt includes the earth element in the water. Keep a towel next to the chair; you will need it to wipe your feet. Once you are ready, follow the guided meditation for today.

Put your feet inside the water and take few deep breaths. Then look at the candle in front of you. Focus on its flame. Meditate while looking at the flame for a few minutes. Whenever your attention wanders, bring it back to the flame. Now close your eyes and visualize, releasing any blocks, discomfort, or disease trapped in your body into the water in the tub. When you are ready, gently open your eyes and wipe your feet.

Action Steps for Today

Walk bare feet when possible. Notice the air and space around you. Try gazing at the sky for a while.

The Turiya state - Thoughtless Awareness

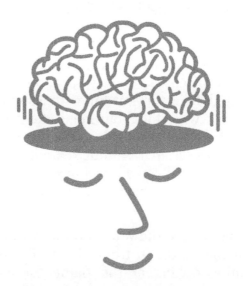

"The quieter you become, the more you are able to hear."

- **Rumi**

Ancient Vedic scriptures describe four states of awareness

1. <u>Jagruti:</u> Jagruti or the waking state is when our body and mind are both active and involved in doing things. They might both (Body and Mind) be focussed on the same

thing (which we call mindfulness) or be involved in totally different things. For example, your mind is wandering or doing aimless thinking while your body is on autopilot.

2. <u>Swapna:</u> Swapna or dreaming state is when our body is at rest, but our mind is continuously dreaming or thinking. This usually happens when we are sleeping. In the dream state, we have access to our subconscious mind, so sometimes dreams may be used to find inspiration or a solution to real-life problems. Although, if you are not yet conscious enough, I would suggest not wasting time trying to find meanings of your dreams.

3. Sushupti: This is the state of a deep sleep when your mind and body are both resting. This state can also be achieved while in a state of deep meditation. Mandukya Upanishad explains that if we can attain the state of Sushupti while awake, we can tap into the prajna, the highest and purest form of wisdom and intelligence.

4. Turiya: Vedic scriptures explain Turiya as the state beyond deep sleep. This is the state which has been described by many spiritual teachers as the state of being one with the self. In this state, the practitioner attains thoughtless awareness, where the mind performs all the karmas (daily duties) but without any aimless thinking. Your actions are not driven by desire but by inspiration. Those who have attained this state can use their thinking mind when needed, but stay free from it at will.

Ancient philosophy defines that a yogi who has attained Turiya awastha (state) is liberated from ego and united with the infinite, all-pervading consciousness. Turiya is the union of atman (individual consciousness) and Brahma (Superconsciousness).

The snake and the rope analogy: Let's understand Turiya by using the famous Snake and Rope analogy. Imagine you walk into a dark room, and you see a brown snake sitting on the bed. Your stress level goes up, and the body reacts exactly like it should when it sees a snake. Suddenly some else comes into the room and switches on the light. You realize that what you thought as the brown snake, is in reality, your brown leather belt. Suddenly all the stress disappears; the body becomes relaxed. You may become a bit embarrassed, but not at all afraid.

Now let's reflect on this story. In the darkness, which is a metaphor for your ego-mind, the snake, which is a metaphor for your ego self, was very real to you. As a result, your fear, which is a metaphor for your life problems, was also very real. But as soon as the light was switched on, the snake was no more real, and you could see more clearly. All your fear disappeared in an instant. Similarly, when one attains the state of Turiya, any sense of a separate egoic identity dissolves, and they become one with the Universe.

Meditation Day 14
The practice of Neti Neti

Neti Neti is a practice used by rishis and yogis in ancient India. It is a Sanskrit term which translates to 'neither this nor that.' It is based on the philosophy that to understand the Brahma (Superconscious) we must first train our brain on what it is not.

Sit down in a comfortable position with your back supported and head free. Take a few deep breaths. Observe what your mind is doing. As the thoughts begin to appear, do not resist or try to control them. Just imagine you are discarding them by saying, 'not this.' Every time a thought pops up, you drop it by saying, 'not this.' As you continue this practice, you will notice the interval between two thoughts slowly increases, and you can remain thoughtless for more extended periods. Meditate like this for a few minutes.

Congratulations on completing Day 14. Your awareness is increasing.

Action Step for Today

Whenever you find yourself overthinking, practice Neti Neti to be in control of your brain.

Connecting Mind Body and Spirit

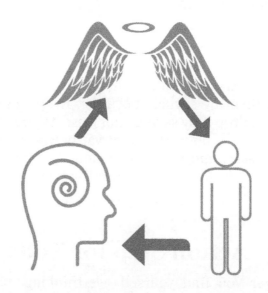

"The body benefits from movement, and the mind benefits from stillness."

— Sakyong Mipham

Most people have an understanding that we have a body, and then our mind is inside our body. But what if I said to you that our body and mind are two separate things using each other effectively to perform tasks in this material world? Our body is what we have. We can touch it, see it, feel it; so, it is as material as it gets. However, I believe we are not our body. We are our mind or, in other words, pure consciousness. And our mind/consciousness may originate from within our body/brain, but it goes beyond it and is far more significant than our body. You can contain your body just like any other physical matter can be contained, but you cannot contain your mind as it is pure consciousness. This concept is often referred to as the 'dualism' of Body and Mind.

How do we define the Mind and Spirit?

There are arguments that even after the body ceases to exist, the mind remains. But because you can not see, touch, or feel the mind, there is no way to prove this. One can use their mind to heal their body (physical health) and brain (mental health). The mind can also be understood as pure awareness. According to ancient philosophy, Spirit is the universal energy that resides in each one of us. Spirit is also associated with heart by some theologists and is thought to be responsible for our sixth senses and intuition. We use our spirit to give and receive real love.

How to enhance the connection between Mind, Body, and Spirit for profound healing?

There are various techniques used to tap into the healing benefits of Mind, Body, and Spirit Connection. Before we dive into some of these techniques, let's discuss the importance of it. Without having a healthy mind, one cannot have a healthy body and vice versa. Ever wondered why a nice shower or massage also helps boost your mood? Similarly, listening to pleasant music or 5 minutes of meditation can have physical benefits. We function as one holistic system of mind, body, and spirit. If you want to see a perfect example of the true connection of mind, body, and spirit, observe a child. When they are unhappy, you can tell clearly by looking at their red face, screams, and tears. On the other hand, when they are happy, you can also tell by their sparkling eyes and rosy cheeks.

Practices such as Yoga and Tai chi are great for tapping into the healing benefits of mind, body spirit connection. Even a nice massage or a shower can help you heal this connection if you put your awareness into it. I am going to guide you through a yoga routine today, which you can do in the morning or evening before meditation to heal your body, mind, and spirit.

Meditation Day 15
Yoga for Wholistic Healing

(a video for this practice is available on the Facebook group. Go to Unit 15)

Lie down on your back, ideally on a hard surface. You can use a yoga mat on the floor. Try to relax your body and mind. Notice your breathing. Count slowly till four as you inhale and till four again as you exhale. Notice the rising and falling sensation in your body. Now slowly bend your knees and bring them to your chest. Continue breathing. Pull your knees as close to your chest as possible. Feel the stretch on your back. Now slowly stretch your leg back to lying position. Now with your eyes closed, turn your head towards your left shoulder as far as it goes. Continue breathing. Feel the stretch in your neck.

Now repeat this towards your right shoulder. Breathing is essential. Bring your head back to the center and take 3-4 deep breathes. Now slowly sit down with your legs folded or on a chair, whatever is comfortable. Wherever your attention goes, your consciousness flows. So take your attention to the center of your heart. Feel your spirit here. Breathe deeply and stay here for some time. Now lift your both hands in front of you as if you are about to hold a ball. Visualize energy flowing through your heart into your hands. Feel this ball of energy. It may help if you try to press it between your palms or move it from one hand to another. Visualize this energy going back into you and expanding to fill your entire body. Feel it expanding outside your body. This is your consciousness. Keep expanding it like a big sphere surrounding your body from all directions. Feel how vast your consciousness is. You will notice that there is no end to it. You can expand it as much as you like. Meditate in this state for 5 minutes.

Congratulations on completing Day 15. You are healing and growing at the same time.

Action Step for Today

Take time out to stretch and breathe a few times during the day. This increases the energy flow between the body and mind.

Energy Healing

"Everything is energy, and that's all there is to it."

- **Albert Einstein**

As science suggests, all matter, including our body, is just vibrating energy. If everything is the energy it must be possible to fix problems in an energy center with more energy. Asian countries have used energy healing for hundreds of years. Reiki, a practice that originated in the early 20th century in Japan, uses energy to heal blocks in the body. Ancient Hindu traditions talk about chakras as energy centers and use chakra clearing techniques for healing body and mind. Acupuncture, an alternative medicine therapy that originated in China around 100BC, uses Meridians, also known as energy superhighways of the body.

Energy healing is based purely on science, and one does not have to be spiritual to benefit from it. Energy is like electricity. Just how you do not see electricity but can still feel it and use it for doing incredible things; you may not be able to see energy, but that should not stop you from using it to supercharge your life. Often when we are trying to fix a problem, we do it on a physical level. But as we know it, it is hard to change the matter or physicality of things. What we need to do is work on the energy level. No matter how much you water the fruits, if the roots don't get enough attention, fruits will soon disappear.

How to benefit from energy healing?

Our bodies are capable of healing themselves. The problem is we do not eat what our bodies were designed to eat, and we do not have a lifestyle that was intended. In most energy practices, the goal is to clear any blocks so that energy can flow freely. We can then bring our awareness into the problem area, so the body sees it as a priority and starts the healing process.

I have found that the best way to use energy healing is in the forms of mini healing meditation throughout the day as and when needed. If anytime you start feeling discomfort in a specific part of your body, or you get overwhelmed with all that is happening around you, just close your eyes and focus on your breathing. Take deep, long breaths. Every time you breathe in, imagine inhaling energy and taking that energy to the part of your body, which is at dis-ease. And when you exhale, imagine you are letting go of any negativity trapped in that part. Regular meditation will enable you to be aware of the blocks even before the problem occurs. Hence, energy healing and meditation go hand in hand.

I will share an energy healing meditation technique at the end of this chapter, which you can use every day or at least once a week to heal your body and mind. If you are suffering from any illness, I would suggest you use this meditation every day. It is important to note that energy healing can work along with your regular medication if you are taking any. Do not stop taking your medicine without consulting your doctor. Some other things you can do to keep your energy levels high is - add some Himalayan salt or Epsom in your bath. Burning sage may also be useful to clear any negative energy around your aura.

Meditation Day 16
Healing Meditation

Sit comfortably with your back supported and head free. Close your eyes and take a few deep breaths. Put your both hands together with fingers and palms touching parallelly to each other. Imagine a vast stream of energy coming down from the sky in the form of white light and is filling your body. Once your body is full, slowly separate your palms to about an inch apart. Feel the vibrational energy between your finger and palms. Continue to take deep breaths.

Next, place your hands on your head. Feel the energy from your hands is healing your brain. Take a few deep breaths. Now place your right hand to the left part of your body, where your neck meets your shoulders. Hold it with a gentle force.

Imagine energy flowing through your right hand and healing the left side of your shoulder and neck. Take a few deep breaths. Next, repeat the same procedure with your left hand on the right side of your neck and shoulder. Take a few deep breaths.

Place your hands on your lower back. Imagine energy flowing through your hands and healing your lower back. Take few deep breaths here. Now rest your hands on your lap. If you are suffering from any health issues, or have any discomfort in your body, place your hands on the problem area. Imagine the energy flowing out of your hands and healing this area. Feel that the problem is improving, and your health is getting better. Take a few deep breaths. Now rest your hands on your lap, and when you are ready, slowly open your eyes.

Action Step for Today

Do quick mental scans of your body throughout the day and place your hands on any areas of discomfort to perform instant energy healing.

Day 17
Managing Stress

"Stress is the trash of modern-day life. If you do not dispose of it properly, it will pile up and overtake your life."

-Danzae Pace

I believe that whenever we are dealing with a problem, we must first ask three questions: What? Why? And How? In the same order. Let's start by discussing What is stress?

I have spoken to many friends, family, colleagues, and clients. Whenever they tell me what is causing them stress, it is one of these reasons:

1. Money - They do not seem to have enough. Surprisingly, some of them earn 1,000 pounds a month, while others earn 10,000 a month, they still both have the same problem.
2. Job or Career – They are not happy with their job or business.
3. Relationships – They are not happy with their relationships in life. This could be with their partners, siblings, parents, or children.
4. Time – This is one thing that gets many people. They never have enough time to do it all.
5. Future – This is the most interesting one. I know a lot of people who have everything but are worried that they will not have it in the future. I call it the What if? Curse. What if the economy is doomed? What if people stop buying my products? What if I lose my job? Etc. You get the point.

What if I told you that all these reasons or any other reason which stresses most people are only due to one thing? You have created an expectation of how things should be, and the things are not going as per your expectation.

To understand what stress does to your body, let's go on time travel. Imagine a time thousands of years ago when we still use to live in Jungles. You are walking through the woods, and suddenly you see a tiger approaching you. The body triggers a stress response and stops doing whatever it's supposed to do to respond to this life or death situation. The brain releases adrenaline and cortisol, aka stress hormones. These are responsible for causing a lot of nuisances in our body, such as insomnia and premature aging. Your heart-rate would go up rapidly to move blood through the body. Blood vessels restrict to allow quicker blood movement, which, as a result, will increase the blood pressure. Blood sugar and blood lipids increase, so there is more energy to move. Circulation to your gut decreases, because digestion is not a priority when a tiger is chasing you. Immune function drops rapidly as the body needs energy to 'fight or flee.'

The stress response is an essential function of the body in a life or death situation. The problem is that we give too much importance to everyday activities in our life. Therefore, our nervous system cannot distinguish between being chased by a tiger and being stuck a traffic Jam.

According to research, 90 % of the total doctor visits are related to problems caused by stress. In the world today, most of us are not living our true potentials as our body is using all the energy to be ready for a fight or flee situation. This, in the long run, causes health problems and lower energy levels.

How to Manage Stress?

Now that we have an understanding of what stress is and why we should learn to manage, I am going to introduce you to two models that you can adopt in your life, never to feel stressed again.

Model 1: Good thing Bad thing who knows

I adopted this model from a beautiful old story of a farmer and his son. Allow me to share this story with you:

Once upon a time, there lived a farmer with his son in a tiny village. The father and son did not have many material possessions. They still lived happily and in content. The villagers soon started to envy them and were always curious to find out the reason for their happiness.

One day the farmer decided to use all his savings to buy a horse. Unfortunately, the very next day, the horse managed to escape and run into the hills. The villagers visited to express their sympathy. They remarked, "How unfortunate you are. What happened is bad." To which the farmer said, "Good thing? Bad thing? Who knows?

A few days later, the horse returned and brought with him another six beautiful horses. The villagers revisited the farmer. This time they said, "How fortunate you are. You lost one horse but got back another six." To which the farmer's reply was the same again, "Good thing? Bad thing? Who knows?

After a few days, the farmer's son fell from one of the horses and broke his leg. Even though his leg healed in some time, the injury left him with a permanent limp. The villagers came to visit again and remarked, "How unfortunate. What happened is bad. Who is going to help you in the fields now?" To which the farmer repeated the same words, "Good thing? Bad thing? who knows?"

Soon after that, a war broke out. It was required for all the young men to join the army. However, the farmer's son was spared due to his limp. The villagers once again came to visit him. They said, "You are so fortunate. Your son gets to stay with you, where we are not sure if our sons will ever return home." The farmer's reply was still the same, "Good thing? Bad thing? Who knows?

And this continues. The moral of the story is that **Stress is a choice,** and if you stop labeling the outcomes in your life as good or bad, then chances are you will start choosing happiness over stress.

Have you ever observed that a past occurrence that had seemed bad at the time turned out to be the good thing or at least not so bad thing when you are looking back at it? What has happened has happened and can not be changed. But how you respond to it is your choice. You can choose to label it bad and increase your suffering, or you can walk away saying, "Good thing? Bad Thing? Who knows?"

Model 2: Focus on your actions and not your results

I adapted this model from one of the most beautiful scriptures of all time – the Bhagavad Gita. Imagine a time when we used to live in the wild. A hunter is trying to shoot a deer with his bow and arrow. The hunter is very skillful and has never missed a target before. Does this guarantee that the hunter will be able to get his goal this time? No, not at all. The hunter has command over his arrow and its direction. The hunter can have command on his focus. But the hunter has no power to control over the deer, who may sense the danger and move at the very last minute. Such is life.

In life, there are things which we can control, and then there are things which we cannot. Most of the time, things do not happen as planned due to reasons beyond our control. It is, therefore, important not to focus too much on the outcome. Instead, put all your focus on your efforts. Do not celebrate your results; celebrate your actions. It may take some time to adopt these models, but once you do, you will never be stressed again.

Meditation Day 17
Meditation to let go

You can do this meditation while lying down or sitting. If you are sitting, sit with your back supported and head free. Forget all the deadlines, problems, and stress for the next ten minutes. Take this opportunity to pause your life. Fall back and relax. Slowly close your eyes and take big, deep breaths. Breathe in and out. As you breathe in, feel your body expanding, and as you breathe out, release any stress or tension in the body and mind. Notice how your body is relaxing every time you breathe out. Do it a few more times. Breathe in and out. Let the thoughts come and go. Meditate in this state for 5-10 minutes. And when you are ready, slowly open your eyes.

Congratulations on completing Day 17. You are moving forward and showing up every day, which is commendable.

Action Step for Today

Anytime you feel stressed during the day, close your eyes and take your attention to your breathing. When you breathe in, feel the body expanding, and when you breathe out, release any stress or tension. Do it at least for three breaths.

Day 18

Human Mind

"You have a brain and mind of your own. Use it and reach your own decisions."

- Napolean Hill

Our mind can do miraculous things beyond imagination yet remains one of the most ignored parts of our being. Notice I said, 'our being' and not 'our body', because our mind is way bigger than our body.

Before we discuss what the mind is?; it's essential that we establish what mind is not. It is not our thought; it is not our brain, and it is not our body. While all these things are part of the feedback mechanism used by the mind, they are not the mind.

What is Mind?

Let's look at how modern science and ancient philosophy defines mind.

Professor Dan Siegal, at UCLA School of Medicine, believes that our mind is not confined to what's inside our skull or even our body. He describes that a critical component of the mind is "the emergent self-organizing process, both embodied and relational, that regulates energy and information flow within and among us."

Based on the ancient yogic system, our mind is made up of four components:

1. **Buddhi** or what we call intellect.
2. **Ahankara** - This is a part of our brain that defines our self-identity.
3. **Manas** or what we understand as Memory.
4. And **Chitta** also understood as consciousness.

Now since most of us are neither scientists nor yogis. I am going to generalize things to create a simple model to understand our minds. I believe that your mind is you. Which also means you are not your brain. This is the main benefit of this model. Most people believe that they are their brain. They then try to muscle down their brain using their brain. I tried it myself; it doesn't work.

So, we have a basic model of what our mind is, and we know that we do not need to manage our mind. Instead, we, our mind, must manage our brain. But why?

Why must we manage our Brain?

Let me do an experiment with you. This requires you to visualize for the next few seconds. Imagine that you are holding a big juicy half slice of lemon in your hand. Try and feel the weight of this lemon. Now take this lemon to your nose. What does it smell like? Next, slowly squeeze this lemon into your mouth.

If you are like most people, you would have noticed that your mouth has started to produce extra saliva. The purpose of this saliva is to neutralize the acid in the lemon juice you just squeezed in your mouth. Even though it's just a simple experiment, it gives a profound message.

According to research conducted at MIT, our brain can not distinguish between real events and our imagination. Your brain will believe what your mind wants it to believe. Since the brain controls every function of your body, you must know how to manage it.

Mind the Brain

Think about your brain as a child. What does a child want? The child in your brain wants to feel safe. It wants to be loved. Its prime objective is to ensure the survival of the body. So, it will automatically want to prevent any situation which gives pain right now, be it that gym class or that Broccoli. It seeks instant gratification rather than long term fulfillment. I am aware that there are many technical faults in this model, but it helps us to understand the attributes of our brain. So please bear with me on this.

Now, what does your Human mind want? Our Human mind thrives on Growth and purpose. It thinks long term. Anything which you set as your goals is what your mind wants. Once you understand that your brain is not you and its attributes are similar to those of a child, it becomes far easier to manage it.

Let's look at four techniques we can use to manage our brain effectively.

1. **Claim those easy wins**
   Win those small battles against your brain, and soon your brain will get used to following instructions. Every morning when the alarm rings, instead of hitting the snooze button, leave the bed before you can count till five. This gives less time for the brain to make excuses. Set the alarm for going to the gym, and as soon as the alarm rings decide, you will not have a dialogue with your brain until you are outside of your house. You cannot win with the brain in an argument because it controls your emotions, and it is far more intelligent. Therefore, it is best to act before you have time to think in these situations.

2. **Motivate your Brain**
   Your brain needs motivation while your mind is driven by inspiration. There is a thing about motivation. It's like a ripple in the water. When you throw a stone in a pond of still water, you will instantly see the formation of numerous ripples. But what happens if you did not throw another stone. The water will become still. Motivation works in a very similar way. Therefore, to keep our brain motivated, we need to make an effort continually. There are two steps you can take to keep your brain motivated:

   a) **Have Positive Conversations.** When having a conversation with your brain or what we call self-chatter, treat as if you were talking to a close friend. It

is evident that if we are not kind to a friend, sooner or later, we will lose that friend. Same is the case with our brains if we are not kind when talking to our brain, soon our brain could start separating itself from us/our mind. This is what leads to depression or, in extreme cases, Dissociative identity disorder.

Imagine if you had a close friend who is continually finding fault in you, and you could not get rid of that friend. Well, if you are criticizing yourself, this is precisely the situation you are putting your brain into.

b) **Feed the right information.** The brain works like a computer. It processes the information it receives and produces emotions and reactions. While it's hard to control our emotions and reactions, we, our mind can filter or chose the information sent to our brain. One good way of doing so is by taking time out every morning to feed positive information to our brain consciously. This could be done by reading a good book or by using affirmations. I have created a morning affirmation audio, which I listen to every morning while having my coffee. You can find it in the same link as your other book bonuses at www.superhumaninyoucom/book-bonus. Remember, it's the feeling which is essential. Just like the lemon experiment, you should feel the affirmation more than you listen to it.

3. Practice the mantra of who Cares?

There was a point in the history of our civilization when all we cared about was food. As long as we got our two meals for the day, we couldn't care less about anything else. The problem with today's information-overloaded world is that we care too much or, as Mark Manson said, "We give too many 'F**ks'" Everything we care about takes a part of our energy. We only have 24 hours in a day and a certain amount of energy, so why waste your cares on things that don't matter to you. There may even be things that matter to you but are not worth caring for. Let's look at some examples. A cashier at the supermarket is rude to you? Is it worth waiting for the manager to complain about him or her? Who cares? You slept in today and missed your gym? Is it worth ruining the rest of your day by carrying this guilt? You can go to the gym tomorrow or in the evening. Who cares? Not caring is not about being irresponsible but quite the opposite. It is about being responsible and having the ability to respond to more critical tasks at hand.

4. **Practice Pause**

Have you ever noticed that if you have too many tabs open on your laptop or computer, it dramatically slows down? Our brain works in a very similar fashion, and every thought is like a tab. During the day, we open so many tabs that our brain is never performing at its full potential. Controlling thoughts could be daunting, and I am sure many of you, including me, have tried and failed.

But what if I told you there is a better way to close these tabs. Remember how we discussed that brain and mind are separate. Thoughts are a conversation between the brain and the mind. Every thought is a dialogue initiated by the mind. Stop the dialogue, and the thoughts will stop. Let me explain it in more simple terms. Mental chatter is we talking to ourselves. So to stop thinking, you just have to stop talking to yourself.

Meditation Day 18
Meditation for Brain Power

Sit comfortably with back supported and head free. Slowly close your eyes and take a few deep breaths. Now take your attention to your forehead just between your eyebrows. Keep your attention here for a few breaths. Now slowly move your focus to the right hemisphere of your brain or right part of your head. Keep your concentration here for a few breaths. Next, move your attention to the left hemisphere of the brain or left part of your head. Keep your attention here for a few breaths. Now slowly bring your attention to the top of your skull. Meditate here for few minutes. When you are ready, slowly open your eyes.

Congratulations on completing day 18. You should be proud of what you have achieved until today.

Action Step for Today

Practice PAUSE for at least 2 minutes every three hours during the day to keep your brain functioning optimally.

Thoughts Lead to Emotions

"Your emotions are the slaves to your thoughts, and you are the slave to your emotions."

— Elizabeth Gilbert

'Emotre' Latin derivative of the word emotion means Energy in Motion. You can feel this yourself. Pay attention to how you feel when you are angry or sad. Is our energy/aura expanding or contracting? Notice the same when you feel happy or grateful. Is your energy/aura expanding or contracting?

Emotions are very powerful. People often say after they did something terrible that they were too emotional, or they lost control of their emotions. Most of us genuinely let emotions run our life, instead of choosing our emotions to run a more fulfilling life. You can often hear people saying, 'I have no control over my emotions' or 'I did such and such cause I was angry or sad.' But what if there was a model you can use to hack your emotions. What if there was a way to chose your emotions? Which emotions would you choose?

Our emotions are the aftermath of our thoughts. Let's understand this with an example – You are driving to work or a meeting one morning. Suddenly someone dangerously overtakes you. What will be your instinct thought? What a jerk? Can he not see? Does he not know how to drive? So impatient? As a result, what will be your emotion? – Anger, Frustration, hatred. Do we not understand why that person was in such a rush? What if you knew that the person driving was rushing to the hospital to see their loved one who was counting their last breath? We don't know, right? What if you could think that this was the case? What will be your emotions after this thought? Compassion, Kindness, Forgiveness. What if we could choose our thoughts based on what emotional state we want to be in? Our emotions affect us more than they affect any other person. In this case, the person who overtook your car is not affected by what you think about him/her; you are.

It is beneficial to reframe situations and use the power of thoughts to feel positive, but it is also important to not judge yourself for feeling in a certain way. When we attach judgment to an emotion, we either try to hide/suppress it, or we fall into the guilt trap. This leads to even more negative emotions. The correct method is to accept the fact that your brain did not like something, and it is communicating it to you by sending energy signals or emotions. Now use your thoughts to reframe the situation. Tell yourself that no matter what happened and who is to blame, I will create action points and note down lessons for things I can do differently. Next, I will reframe the situation to create 'my version of the story,' which supports my mental health and productivity.

Remember that being emotional is not a bad thing. It means your system is working correctly. If you do not feel emotions, it might mean that there is something wrong with your beliefs or the way your brain is operating. This can lead to more significant problems in the long run. When you make progress in meditation, you will notice that you feel stronger emotions, as you are more present, and your body and mind are in sync. This is perfectly fine. What we need to be mindful of is how we are responding to these emotions.

Meditation Day 19
Meditation for Emotional Balance

Sit comfortably with back supported and head free. Gently close your eyes and take a few deep breaths. Now, remember an event from the past which affected you. Recall the event and let any emotions come out. Do not resist anything but also don't get carried away. Just observe different feelings. It is essential to accept your emotions first before you can let them go. Once you have felt the emotion and acknowledged it, its time to let it go. Take a few deep breaths. As you exhale, release the emotion and associated pain from the body. If you want, you can repeat the same process with another event. Otherwise, just focus on your breath and meditate for a few minutes.

Action Step for the day

Whenever you are feeling an unwanted emotion, remind yourself that emotions are just energy signals initiated by your brain to communicate whether it likes or dislikes something. Once you have received the message, the need for that emotion is finished. Acknowledge the emotion that you are feeling a certain way. Commit to yourself that you are going to do something about it if it's in your control. Breathe into it and then let it go as you breathe out, while also visualizing that your energy is expanding as you breathe out.

Manifesting: The Art of Bending Reality

"The day science begins to study non-physical phenomena; it will make more progress in one decade than in all the previous centuries of its existence."

- **Nikola Tesla**

The art of bending Reality is not a new concept. The word was first coined in the biography of Steve Jobs written by

Walter Isaacson. In the book, Isaacson explains Jobs' ability to bend reality in his mind and in the mind of others. T Harv Ecker, the author of 'Secrets of Millionaire mind,' said, "What you focus on Expands." According to Ronda Byrne, the creator of the famous movie 'The Secret' – "Your thoughts become things."

Let me explain this by sharing a story with you. There was once a man called David, who was tired of his stressful life. Nothing ever went his way, so he decided he will go to this mystical island and find 'inner peace' (whatever that means). When he reached the island, he started looking for a place; he could make his base. The sun was shining high in the sky, and the scorching heat was becoming unbearable. As David kept walking, feelings of doubt began to creep in his mind. He thought to himself, "Is this island really mystical?"; "Did I make a stupid mistake to come here?" His mouth started to become dry, and breathing was getting difficult. He thought to himself, "Wouldn't it be nice if I could get some water?" After a few steps, David saw a stream of freshwater. He quickly put his bag on the side and quenched his thirst, and continued to walk. Soon after, he started to feel hungry and thought to himself, "Wouldn't it be nice if I could get some food?" To his surprise, as he walked a few steps, he saw a table with all kinds of delicious food on it. He looked around, but there was no one in sight, so he decided to fulfill his hunger. He thought to himself, "What a COINCIDENCE?"

Once David was done eating, he continued to walk again, but it wasn't too long until he started feeling tired. The sun was still blazing in the sky, so he thought to himself, "Wouldn't it be nice if I could find a tree so that I can rest in its shed?" Suddenly he sees a big banyan tree within a short walk away. The man became delighted and thanked his 'LUCK.' But as he was lying down under the tree, the feelings of DOUBT started to creep again. He reflected everything which had happened in the day and started to feel FEAR in his chest. He thought, "How could all this have happened? What if there is a Devil at this place?" The next moment he saw a big monster approaching him from a short distance. He jumped up and became even more FEARFUL. He thought again, "Oh No! this monster is going to eat me." Do you know what happened next? That's right; he got eaten by the monster. What if I told you that our Universe is very similar to this mystical island and often gives us anything we focus on. However, there are two fundamental rules.

Rule 1: The first rule is that you will not get what you want or ask for instantly; there will always be a time gap. Imagine if you had the privilege to get anything you want as soon as you want it. You would think of a tiger, and the next moment you see a tiger walking in the room. So, this rule is actually for our good. As often, and especially when overpowered by our emotions, we wish for things that we don't really want. Due to this rule, most of us feel that things never work in our way, or we never get what we want. When the actual reason is, we don't want something long enough for Universe to act on it.

Imagine you are sitting in a Michelin star restaurant. The waiter comes to take your order, and you place an order of Carrot and Coriander soup with some bread on the side. The waiter takes the order in the kitchen, and the Chef starts working on it. Chef chooses the fresh and best quality carrots and coriander to put in your soup. He cuts them nicely and puts them in some water to boil along with some other spices. It is now 20 minutes since you have placed your order, and you are starting to get impatient. Meanwhile, in the Kitchen, the Chef is cooking your soup on a slow flame to get the best flavors. It is now 30 minutes since you have been waiting, you get annoyed and asked the waiter to change your order.

You say to him that soup is taking too long, you want to change your order to potato and vegetables instead. The waiter goes in the kitchen, tells the chef, and the chef who was just about to pour your soup in the serving bowl now pours your soup down the drain, and starts preparing potatoes and vegetables for you. With the same process, the chef begins choosing the best ingredients for you and starts cooking your meal. Half an hour goes by, and this time you get even more annoyed and change your order again. The chef who had almost finished making your potatoes and vegetables puts them on the side and starts preparing your new order. Can you see why you are unable to get what you want? Can you see how, because you were not willing to wait for more than half an hour, now you have to wait almost two hours or forever? It is, therefore, imperative to take time to figure out what you want and, once decided, keep your focus on it until you get it. FOCUS is Following One Cause Until Successful.

Rule 2: The Universe listens to your emotions and actions more than your words. Suppose you want to be a world-class public speaker, but in your mind, you are continually thinking about everything which could go wrong when you are on stage. What would the universe listen to? The universe will listen that you are afraid to be on stage, and so will make sure you do not get there, or in case if you do get there, it will make sure you do not get there again. Your thoughts and beliefs will dictate your emotions. Therefore, think of constructive thoughts to have supportive emotions. A good practice is to observe your thoughts always and swap them for a more supportive one. You will notice I said supportive, not positive. Cause when you classify your thoughts or anything for that matter into positives and negatives, you are using your judgment, and judgment will lead to attachment. We do not want to be attached to our thoughts; we want to be separate from them, to manage them better. Emotions, as we have discussed on Day 19, are Energy in Motion. So, when you align your energy and action towards what you want to achieve, you will become the master creator of your reality (in time, of course). As you master your emotions, the time gap will reduce too.

Think about the Placebo effect. And if you have not heard of the term before or are a bit skeptical about it, you should watch the videos in the book bonuses section of the website at www.superhumaninyou.com/book-bonus. Our body and mind can do incredible things. However, our brain is not so good at identifying what is real or unreal. Remember the lemon experiment we did on Day 18. Your brain will believe whatever you tell it. This is a fantastic quality of our powerful brain. It trusts us without asking questions. Use this quality to support your growth, and you will soon start Bending Reality.

Meditation Day 20
Manifest a New Reality.

Sit down comfortably with your back supported and head free. The first step is to close your eyes and focus on your breathing. This is when you have your attention within you. Now slowly take your attention outside in front of you without opening your eyes. Next, we will focus on creating three images step by step:

1. Think about why do you want what you want? This is where you must feel the pain. Research has shown that if you start your visualization by experiencing your current pain and being honest about it, then the process will be more effective. So if its better health you are after. Experience how you feel not having good health. Imagine things you are missing out. The

emotions which you feel in this first step will help you establish that connection and are going to propel you towards the desired outcome. Although, do not get carried away, instead take the audience seat and observe everything for less than a minute.

2. Now, imagine a vast stream of white light from the sky, like rainfall, is erasing this situation from your life, just like the darkness goes away as soon as you switch on the lights.

3. At last, imagine the light has disappeared, and what you see next is a new reality, the one you want to create. Remember, the best way to connect with your subconscious mind is through emotions, so feel as if you already have what you are trying to achieve. Feel how you feel. Try and involve all the senses. If it is health you seek, visualize yourself in perfect shape or form. Visualize yourself doing things that you could not have done without having this new healthy body. Imagine where you are? Are you in a park, on the beach? Can you feel the air? What do you smell? If your goal is to become wealthier, Imagine things like what car are you driving? Which country are you in? It is also helpful to visualize how what you have achieved is going to help others? Like your loved ones or society. Feel their joy. Now you can open the eyes and come out of the meditation

Congratulations on completing Day 20. You are just a day less to completing your challenge.

Action Step for Today

Observe your mind throughout the day and pay attention to any signs of fear or doubts. Whenever you notice any such emotion, meditate on it and release it from your body.

Day 21
Surrender your way to Enlightenment

"Surrender is like a fish finding the current and going with it."

- **Mark Nepo**

If you tell any man/woman of the 21st century that surrender is the only way to salvation, they will look back at you as if you are some loser. After all, our society teaches us to be go-getters, never to give up, and be the warrior who has burnt his boats. But what if I told you that you could be a warrior and fully surrender at the same time. There is only a small difference between a warrior and a raging bull; A warrior has a purpose. Surrendering, in a spiritual sense, does not mean giving up. No, not at all. Instead, it means giving up anything which is not aligned to your purpose.

In society today, we have so many management courses that every one of us has become an excellent manager but a miserable human being. To be a good Human being, we just need to focus more on being and less on doing. Practice more of surrender and less of micromanaging or controlling. We are free spiritual beings and not time-controlled robots. Don't get me wrong it is essential to have goals aligned to your life's purpose. I believe that every one of us must try to live our full potential. Have all those beautiful things we want to experience and help as many people as we can. However, micromanagement kills brilliance in us.

Do all you have to do, but with surrender. Bhagavad Gita explains Surrender as one's detachment from the results of their action. This is also referred to as the supreme form of yoga. Detachment from your results does not mean that you stop taking action. Instead, detachment allows you to focus wholly on your efforts without worrying about the results. It gives you the freedom to fail and learn as winning and losing is no more your worry. Now let's look at this argument from a logical viewpoint. What happens when you get detached from the results of your actions – You win over your fear of losing. Fear is the single biggest reason why 98% of us are living an ordinary life with an extraordinary soul.

Have you ever found yourself in a mental state where no matter how hard you work or how much you do, you feel that you should do more? A situation where you feel like you have to be on constant guard or else something will go wrong? Or the fear that something terrible might happen? Well, whatever you fear will appear. Surrender is the only way to end all worries. It is putting an end to that restlessness, which may be keeping you up at night. It's not the end of taking actions, but the end of worrying about the results of your actions or inactions.

When we free ourselves of our fears, it becomes easier to access the alpha waves of the brain. Research suggests that alpha waves are more prominent when our brain is calm and at a resting state. Surrendering means end of resistance. Therefore, surrendering helps increase alpha wave activity in our brains. Alpha waves can dramatically boost our creativity and problem-solving skills. Creativity requires taking a path that has never been taken; it requires freedom; it requires ignoring the norms. This is another reason why surrendering might supercharge your creative genius. Surrendering means giving up control and setting your mind free. It nudges you to set free any hate, grudges, or judgment you have stored in your memory, so there is more space in your brain's workshop.

Sometimes we put too much focus on being right that we sacrifice our happiness for the sake of it. Changing the world is not our responsibility; changing us is. In conflicts over things that have nothing to do with your purpose in life, it is best to surrender than to fight. Choose your battles and surrender to those that are not worth fighting. Then use the saved energy to propel you towards what matters.

True surrender is about letting go, and about accessing flow. It is about putting all your focus on your actions and having an unshakable faith and belief that whatever the Universe brings to you as a result of those actions is for your best.

Meditation Day 21
Surrender to The Universe

If you have trouble sleeping, you will find this meditation helpful. Practice it just before bedtime. When you are ready, lie down comfortably on a mat or your bed. Close your eyes and take a few deep breaths.

Visualize, you are walking up a cliff. As you walk, drop all distractions, stress, and worries. Drop any urgency of doing things. Visualize taking your phone out of your pocket, switching it off, and dropping this too. Notice how light you feel. Notice the cold wind touching your skin. You have reached the end of the cliff, and you can see the vast ocean below. You can see a beautiful sunset in front of you. This is the time for you to drop all your fear and doubts. Trust that the Universe is there to support you and take a leap of faith. Step forward and let it go. Let it all go.

Allow yourself to fall freely. Feel air rushing through your hair and past your body. You have nothing to resist, nothing to fear, and nothing to attend. You are in a complete state of surrender. Meditate at this moment for few breaths. Your body has reached the surface of the ocean now. As you touch the surface, you realize that the sea is gentle and supportive. Your body goes under the surface of the sea and comes back to the surface. Feel your body floating on the surface of the water. Meditate in this state for a few minutes.

Action Step for Today

Do at least one thing today by just following your intuition or gut feeling and without judgment or analysis. Do this with full surrender and be prepared to accept the result with gratitude no matter what it is. Notice how it feels.

Conclusion

Congratulations on finishing the 21 Day Challenge. You have proved to yourself that you are committed to your growth and are willing to move forward in life, subsiding all doubts and fears.

You may be thinking what next? I have introduced you to different styles of meditations in a short and simple way. I believe each of us is different and respond to situations differently. There is no one-size-fits-all meditation. Choose the meditation style that suits you, and gets you results. Try them. You can also mix and match different styles. For example, I do a ten minutes meditation every morning, where I start with reciting a mantra three times, then do a creative visualization that combines the elements of compassion, forgiveness, gratitude, and manifesting. I do short one-minute mindfulness routines every three hours during the day. And at night, I practice surrender while I am on my bed, ready to sleep. I do healing meditations on the weekends, which includes energy healing and five-element meditation. You can find the complete guided routine for my meditations by visiting www.superhumaninyou.com/book-bonus.

This book, along with your bonuses on the website is all you need to build a solid meditation ritual. Although, if you still want to explore further and want to take your practice to the next level, I invite you to enroll in **The Power Within – Second Phase** course on the website. My intention in offering this course is not to upsell you anything. It is just to support you if you think you need more support.

Finally, I have included two bonus chapters on the following pages. Please go through them. They cover great points to accelerate the benefits of your meditation practice.

I am thankful that you chose to purchase this book, and I hope it was able to deliver more than your expectations. Please review the book if you get time. Gift it to your family and friends. Talk about it on social media. Let's get more people meditating.

My best wishes to you

Anurag

The Power of Rituals

"We first make our habits; then our habits make us."

-   **John Dryden**

The Chinese Bamboo tree, one of the tallest trees, takes five years to grow its roots. It doesn't break through the ground until 5th year. But when it does come out, it only takes five months for it to grow 90 feet tall—our habits work in a very similar fashion. At first, the change in your performance or productivity may seem insignificant, but slowly the results start compounding. This is also true for bad habits. At first, it may seem that we are still young, or it's not affecting us. But after some time, when the adverse effects start showing up, they compound rapidly.

You may be wondering why we are talking about habits in a meditation book. Two reasons. First, as I warned you, I am not your traditional meditation teacher, and hence I do not have to follow the norm. Second I feel this topic is critical to this subject as it will help you form a lifelong habit of practicing meditation.

Difference between Rituals and habits

When you do something about the same time in a similar way and under the same environment every day, the practice is called a ritual. And when you perform a ritual for several days without fail, the ritual becomes a habit. It becomes a part of who you are. In a nutshell, rituals are a compelling way to change your life.

Rituals are not only beneficial for forming good habits; they are also a potent tool to keep us in the right frequency and mindset. Behavioral scientist Michael Norton notes that "every culture—and throughout history— people who perform rituals report feeling better." When we finish a ritual, it gives the brain a feeling of happiness, satisfaction, and winning. If you incorporate three-morning rituals as part of your morning routine, you have had three wins even before starting the day. Soon you will notice that these smaller wins will transpire into anything big or small you are trying to achieve.

Every time we make a decision, we have to exercise will power and use our brain. After a number of decisions, our brain loses the capability to make the same quality of decisions. Psychologists refer to this as decision fatigue. This is the primary reason why most successful people have weird rituals. For example, Mark Zuckerburg, just like Steve Jobs, wears the same colored t-shirt every day. Tim Kendall, CEO of Pinterest, starts his mornings with an ice bath every day.

Rituals increase our self-confidence. In a world where everything is uncertain, rituals ensure us that there is a part of our life that is still in our control. The reason why rituals work is that they are driven by commitment and a sense of identity. When you start a ritual, your brain adopts it as part of your identity, and hence you are more likely to stick to it.

Bonus Chapter 2
Four Levels of Consciousness

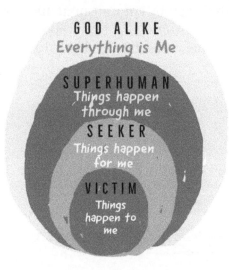

GOD ALIKE
Everything is Me

SUPERHUMAN
Things happen
through me

SEEKER
Things happen
for me

VICTIM
Things
happen to
me

Albert Einstein once said, *"No problem can be solved from the same level of consciousness that created it."*, which implies that we must raise our consciousness to erase our problems. But what is consciousness and how to raise it?

As per the dictionary, Consciousness means the state of being aware and responsive to one's surroundings. The key phrase here is the state of being aware. You can not raise your consciousness unless you are aware. Many modern scientists believe that consciousness can not be defined in terms of time, space, mass, or energy, which may imply that consciousness existed even before these things. Nothing would ever exist if there was no awareness or consciousness. We make sense of the world around us based on the level of our consciousness. Nothing in the world has meaning apart from the meaning we give it.

I believe that there are four levels of consciousness. Most of us can operate in two or sometimes even three levels in different situations. Let's discuss this in more detail:

Level 1 – Victim Mode

People at this level believe that everything is happening to them. If you find yourself starting a sentence with - only if, but, or because of this, there are high chances that you are operating at the victim level. Only if I had more time, but I am too old or too young, because of my partner, I cannot focus. At this level, we are always busy pointing out what should change? Outside activities, events, or people determine our actions. We never act; we react.

Level 2 – Seeker Mode

At this level, you start looking for answers. You believe that things happen for you. When you operate at this level, you become curious instead of passing judgments. You begin to understand the laws of the universe. You believe that everything that happens in your life is for you to learn and grow. You take responsibility for your action. Other people, situations, or events do not influence your actions. You act; not react. Instead of focussing on what should change, you ask a better question - How can I change?

Level 3 – Superhuman

I like to call this superhuman level. At this level, you believe that everything that is happening in your life is through you. You are in charge of all that is happening. Most brilliant minds on the planet operate at this level. This is when your inner state becomes unfuckwithable. No person, event, or situation can disturb your inner peace. You become limitless, compassionate, grateful, and a creative genius. You take responsibility for not just your actions but also your inactions. At this state, you are always connected and in the flow. Your consciousness becomes so powerful that you start bending reality.

Level 4 – God alike

The last level is what I refer to as god alike. At this level, you become one with the Universe or Superpower. You believe that everything is you. Some of us may have experienced this state for a short while. Such short experiences are what we call Satori moments. However, it requires constant practice and often years of meditation to be able to attain this state truly. Yogis referred to this state as Samadhi. Sufis called it Turiya. And some prefer the word Enlightenment.

About the Author

Anurag Rai is the founder of Superhuman In You, an organization with a mission to make wisdom available to all. Superhuman University offers courses and content to help individuals grow physically, mentally, and spiritually.

Anurag is also an accountant, property investor, a certified meditation practitioner, entrepreneur, and dad to a five-year-old. He is now on a mission to help entrepreneurs live a happier, stress-free, and fulfilled life. This book is an attempt towards that mission.

To find out more about Anurag, visit

www.superhumaninyou.com/anurag-rai

Email: anurag.rai@superhumaninyou.com

Resources to Help

Website: www.superhumaninyou.com

Enroll Now
Courses: www.superhumanuniversity.org.uk

Facebook: www.facebook.com/limitless.superhuman

SUBSCRIBE
Youtube: www.youtube.com/c/superhumaninyou